Science K
Student Guide

Part 2

At Stride, Inc. (NYSE: LRN) – formerly K12 Inc. – we are reimagining lifelong learning as a rich, deeply personal experience that prepares learners for tomorrow. Since its inception, Stride has been committed to removing barriers that impact academic equity and to providing high-quality education for anyone—particularly those in underserved communities. The company has transformed the teaching and learning experience for millions of people by providing innovative, high-quality, tech-enabled education solutions, curriculum, and programs directly to students, schools, the military, and enterprises in primary, secondary, and post-secondary settings. Stride is a premier provider of K–12 education for students, schools, and districts, including career learning services through middle and high school curriculum. Providing a solution to the widening skills gap in the workplace and student loan crisis, Stride equips students with real world skills for in-demand jobs with career learning. For adult learners, Stride delivers professional skills training in healthcare and technology, as well as staffing and talent development for Fortune 500 companies. Stride has delivered millions of courses over the past decade and serves learners in all 50 states and more than 100 countries. The company is a proud sponsor of the Future of School, a nonprofit organization dedicated to closing the gap between the pace of technology and the pace of change in education. More information can be found at stridelearning.com, K12.com, destinationsacademy.com, galvanize.com, techelevator.com, and medcerts.com.

978-1-60153-329-6

Printed by Bradford & Bigelow, Newburyport, MA, USA, May 2021.

Table of Contents

Student Worksheets and Assessments

Unit 15: Astronomy

Student Guide
Lesson 1: What About Weather?

Learn about different types of weather, from sunny to stormy. Discover how a thermometer can tell us important information about the temperature outside. Observe weather conditions and give your own weather reports. Understand how to prepare and dress for different kinds of weather.

Lesson Objectives

- Identify different weather conditions.
- Record weather conditions on a weather chart.
- Determine the appropriate clothing for different weather conditions.

PREPARE

Approximate lesson time is 45 minutes.

Advance Preparation

- For this science lesson, you will need to collect clothes or other items that would be worn in different weather conditions such as a swimsuit, shorts, tank tops, and sandals for hot weather; jackets, scarves, gloves, thermals, and sweatshirts for cold weather; an umbrella, a raincoat and galoshes for wet weather, etc. Put the clothes in a laundry basket. They can be of all different sizes as long as your student can put them on.

Materials

For the Student
- 🖳 Dress for Weather
- 🖳 My Weather Chart
- crayons, 16 or more - green and red
- envelope
- glue sticks
- scissors, round-end safety

Optional
- paper, 8 1/2" x 11"
- tape, clear
- thermometer
- basket - laundry
- clothing - for warm and cold weather
- pencils, no. 2

Keywords and Pronunciation

temperature : How hot or cold something is. You have to wear a coat today because the temperature is very cold outside.

weather : What it is like outside. Sometimes the weather outside can be sunny, windy, rainy, snowy, hot, or cold.

wind : Moving air. The wind was so strong that it blew my hat off my head.

LEARN
Activity 1: The Weather Outside *(Online)*

Activity 2: My Weather Chart *(Online)*
Safety
Caution your student to use care when handling a thermometer. The glass at the bulb is very thin and could possibly break. Children should not use a mercury thermometer.
Never leave your student unattended outside.

Activity 3: Dress for Weather *(Online)*

ASSESS
Lesson Assessment: What About Weather? (*Online*)
Sit with an adult so that they may review the assessment questions with you.

LEARN
Activity 4. Optional: Watch a Weather Forecast *(Online)*

My Weather Chart

Cut

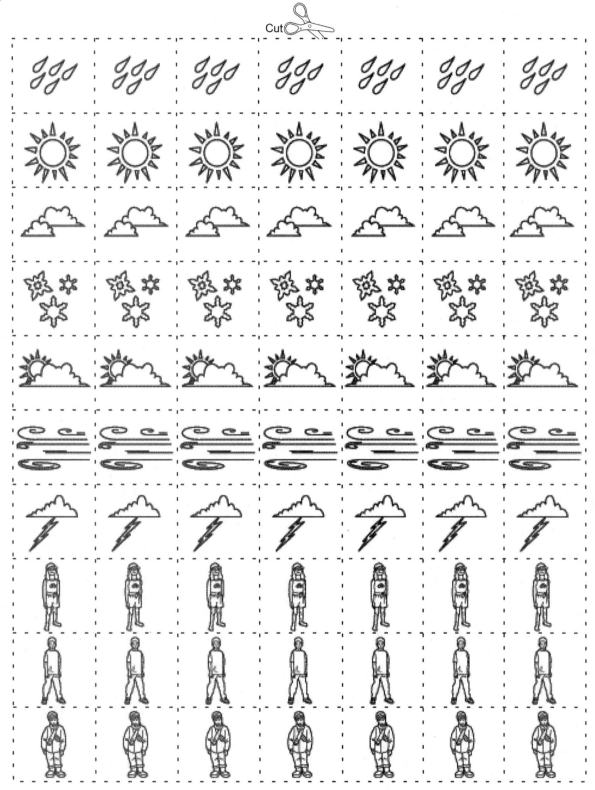

Name _____   Date _____   5

My Weather Chart

Day_____Date_____

weather	temperature

Day_____Date_____

weather	temperature

Day_____Date_____

weather	temperature

Day_____Date_____

weather	temperature

Day_____Date_____

weather	temperature

Day_____Date_____

weather	temperature

Name _____   Date _____

Dress for Weather

Connect each person to the right kind of weather.

Lesson Assessment

What About Weather?

Part 1

This assessment is based on the *My Weather Chart* activity. Review your student's responses on the activity and input the results online.

1. **Prepare**

   Have you ever watched a weather report on television? Weather forecasters tell you what the weather will be like outside by using symbols. Why is it helpful to know what the weather will be like?

   Point to the sun and ask what the weather will be like on that day. Discuss each symbol in turn.

   Investigate

   Tell your student that he will be making observations about the day's weather at the beginning of each lesson.

   Give him the My Weather Chart printout. Have him write his name at the top of the Weather Chart. Mark today as Day 1, and write the date on the chart. Look at the symbols and name the type of weather that each picture shows. Help your student cut out the symbols.

   1. Have your student look outside and describe what the weather is like.
   2. Ask him to choose the symbol that best fits the weather today. Glue the symbol on his chart.
   3. Help your student choose the picture of the person that best describes the temperature for today. Glue it next to his weather symbol.

   Place the remaining pictures in the envelope for the next time.

Part 2

1. What are some words you can use to describe the weather?

2. What is the weather like today?

3. Which picture shows how someone could dress in hot, sunny weather?

4. What kind of clothing could you wear in cold, snowy weather?

Student Guide
Lesson 2: The Sun's Up

Lesson Objectives

- Record weather conditions on a weather chart.
- Explain that the sun is a source of warmth.
- Demonstrate that the sun warms water and that the water goes into the air.
- Record weather conditions on a weather chart.

PREPARE

Approximate lesson time is 45 minutes.

Materials

For the Student

    📖 My Weather Chart

    crayons, 16 or more - red and green (2)

    paper, 8 1/2" x 11"

    thermometer

    glass, drinking (2)

    penny - any coin (2)

    spoon (2)

    plastic sandwich bags, zipper-closed

    towels, paper (2)

Optional

    jar - identical (2)

    lid, jar

    marker, black permanent, non-toxic

    lamp - 60 watt bulb or higher

    plastic wrap

    rubber bands

    tape, masking

    📖 The Sun's Up

    salt - 1/4 cup

    brush, watercolor - paintbrush

    food coloring

    measuring cup

    water - 1/4 cup, warm

LEARN
Activity 1: Weather Observations *(Online)*

Activity 2: The Sun's Warmth *(Online)*
Safety
Use caution when handling glass. At the conclusion of the investigation, test to make sure the objects are not too hot before your student touches them.

Activity 3: Where Does the Water Go? *(Online)*

Activity 4. Optional: The Sun at Work *(Online)*

ASSESS
Lesson Assessment: The Sun's Up (*Online*)
You will complete an offline assessment covering the main objectives of this lesson. Your learning coach will score this assessment.

LEARN
Activity 5. Optional: Salt Water Painting *(Online)*

My Weather Chart

Cut

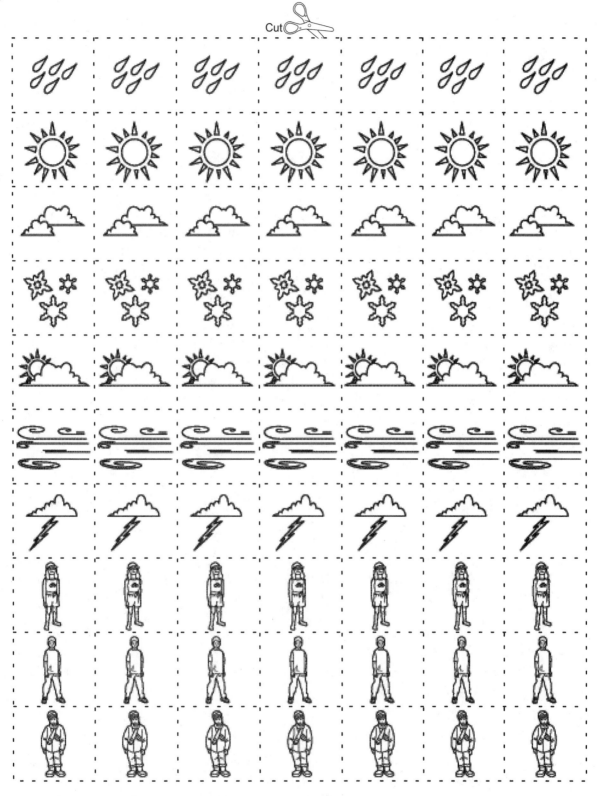

Name _____   Date _____

My Weather Chart

Day _____ Date _____

weather	temperature

Day _____ Date _____

weather	temperature

Day _____ Date _____

weather	temperature

Day _____ Date _____

weather	temperature

Day _____ Date _____

weather	temperature

Day _____ Date _____

weather	temperature

Name _____

Date _____

The Sun's Up

Color the clothes that will dry the fastest.

If you were cold, where would you want to be, in the sun or the shade? Draw a picture of yourself in the spot where you could warm up.

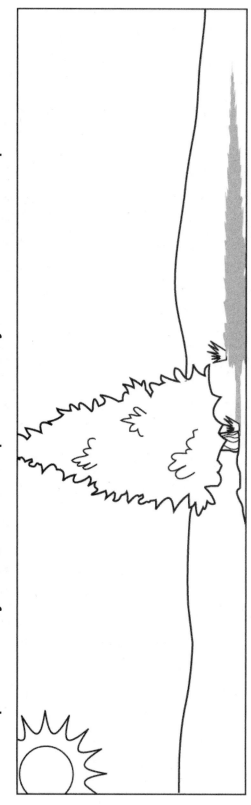

Lesson Assessment

The Sun's Up

Questions:

1. If you leave a crayon outside on a warm, sunny day how will it feel when you go back out to get it, warm or cold?

2. Pretend you just went swimming at the beach and your bathing suit was all wet. What would happen to your suit after you got out of the water and played in the sun for a while?

3. When you hang your wet towel up after a bath, where does the water go as the towel dries?

4. Look at your Weather Chart. Is the weather the same today as it was the last time you checked the weather?

Student Guide
Lesson 3: As the Wind Blows

Lesson Objectives

- Learn that wind is moving air.
- Demonstrate how wind (moving air) can move objects.
- Use a windsock to observe the wind.

PREPARE

Approximate lesson time is 45 minutes.

Advance Preparation

- For this science lesson, you may want to do a trial run of the first investigation. Since hair dryers vary, it might be helpful to test your hair dryer on some of the objects so that when your student does the investigation, he holds the hair dryer an appropriate distance from the objects being tested.

Materials

For the Student
Optional

    ⌨ My Weather Chart

       bottle, plastic - 1 full, 1 empty (2)

       cotton balls (3)

       leaf (3)

       ball - 1 large, 1 small (2)

       household items - hair dryer

       newspaper - sheet

       penny

       water

       1-hole punch

       paper, colored construction, 12"x12"

       tissue paper

       markers, colored, 8 or more

       stapler

       tape, clear

🖥 Wind at Work

 pencils, no. 2

 clay - small piece

 straws, drinking

 tray, Styrofoam, clean

 tub

 paper

 scissors, round-end safety

 play equipment - kite

Keywords and Pronunciation

wind : moving air: The wind could be heard blowing through the trees.

LEARN
Activity 1: Weather Observations *(Online)*

Activity 2: Wind is Moving Air *(Online)*
Safety
Do not use the hair drier or other electrical appliances near water. Use caution when changing heat settings on the dryer so that the air from the dryer is not too hot.

Activity 3: See How It Blows! *(Online)*

Activity 4. Optional: Wind at Work *(Online)*

ASSESS

Lesson Assessment: As the Wind Blows (*Online*)

You will complete an offline assessment covering the main objectives of this lesson. Your learning coach will score this assessment.

LEARN

Activity 5. Optional: Household Draft Walk *(Online)*

Activity 6. Optional: Sailing, Sailing *(Online)*

Activity 7. Optional: Go Fly a Kite! *(Online)*

My Weather Chart

Cut

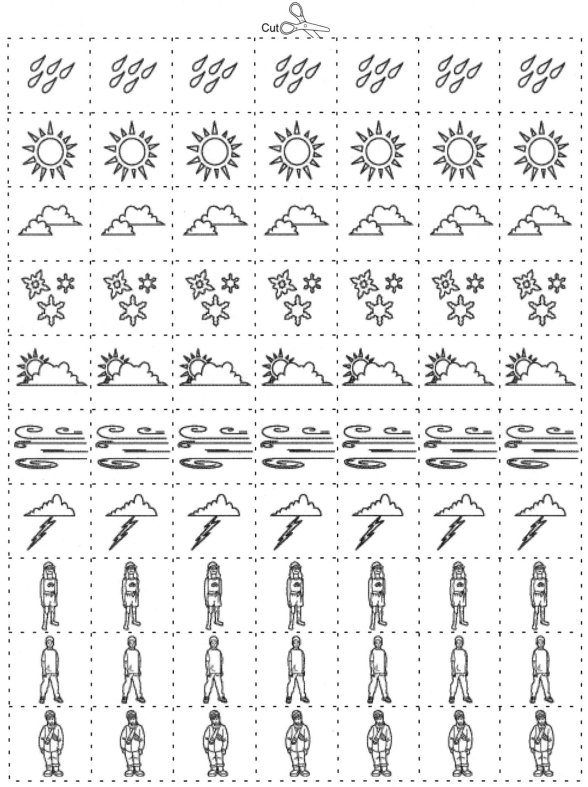

Name _____   Date _____

My Weather Chart

Day_____Date_____   Day_____Date_____

weather	temperature

weather	temperature

Day_____Date_____   Day_____Date_____

weather	temperature

weather	temperature

Day_____Date_____   Day_____Date_____

weather	temperature

weather	temperature

Name

Date

Wind at Work

Color the things being moved by the wind. Which way is the wind blowing?
Color the arrow at the bottom of the page that shows the direction of the wind.

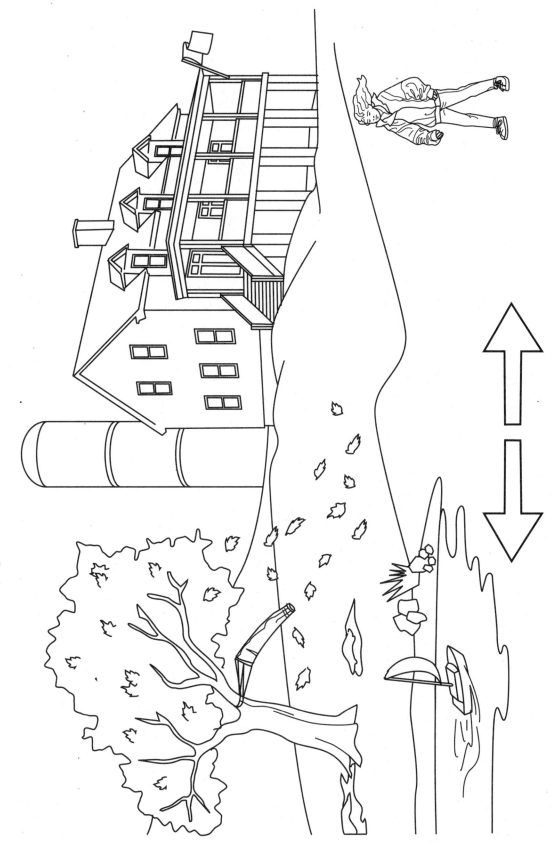

Lesson Assessment

As the Wind Blows

Questions:

1. What would cause the girl's hair, the wind sock, and the leaves to move?

2. What is another name for "moving air?"

3. How can you tell that the wind is blowing outside?

4. Draw a windsock and streamers with no wind blowing. Next to it, draw a windsock that shows the wind blowing a little bit.

Student Guide
Lesson 4: Watching the Clouds Go By

Lesson Objectives

- Know that clouds come in many different shapes, sizes, and colors.
- Know that clouds are made of water.
- Know that clouds are moved by the wind.
- Know that different types of clouds are associated with different types of weather.

PREPARE

Approximate lesson time is 45 minutes.

Materials

For the Student

    🖥 My Weather Chart

    🖥 Cloud Camera Cutout

    🖥 Clouds I See

    1-hole punch

    cardboard, sheets

    cotton balls

    crayons, 16 or more

    paper, colored construction, 12"x12" - dark blue

    Elmer's Glue-All

    paper, 8 1/2" x 11"

    scissors, round-end safety

    yarn - 70 cm

Optional

    🖥 Clouds and Weather

    "It Looked Like Spilt Milk" by Charles G. Shaw

    "The Cloud Book" by Tomie dePaola

Keywords and Pronunciation

wind : moving air: The wind could be heard blowing through the trees.

LEARN
Activity 1: Weather Observations *(Online)*

Activity 2: Cloud Watchin' *(Online)*
Safety
Never look directly into the sun. It can damage your eyes.

Activity 3. Optional: Cloud and Weather Match-Up *(Online)*

ASSESS
Lesson Assessment: Watching the Clouds Go By (*Online*)
You will complete an offline assessment covering the main objectives of this lesson. Your learning coach will score this assessment.

LEARN
Activity 4. Optional: Reading About Clouds *(Online)*

My Weather Chart

Cut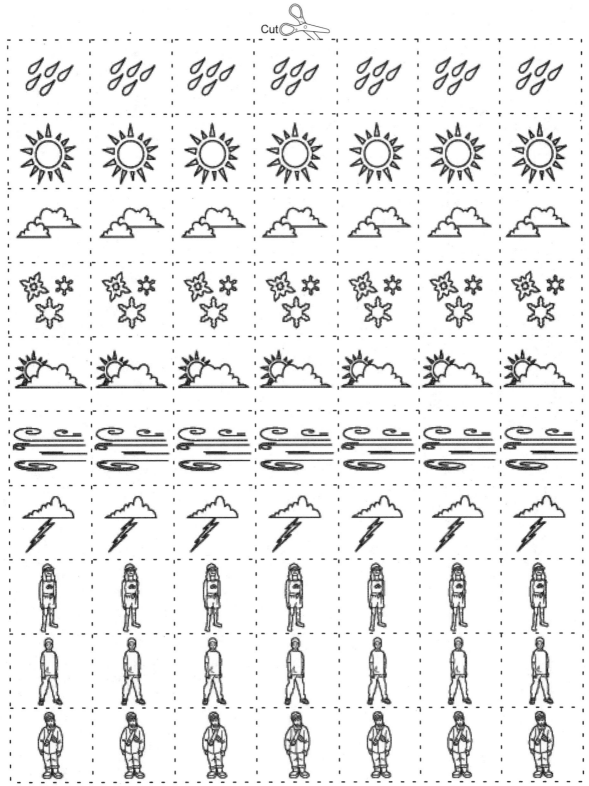

Name _____   Date _____

My Weather Chart

Day_____Date_____   Day_____Date_____

weather ☀️	temperature 🌡️

weather ☀️	temperature 🌡️

Day_____Date_____   Day_____Date_____

weather ☀️	temperature 🌡️

weather ☀️	temperature 🌡️

Day_____Date_____   Day_____Date_____

weather ☀️	temperature 🌡️

weather ☀️	temperature 🌡️

Name

Date

Clouds I See

Look at the clouds in the sky. Circle all the types of clouds you see today.

Cloud Camera Cutout

Cut out the camera. Glue the camera to a piece of cardboard or poster board. Cut a hole in the viewer part of the camera. Punch a hole in each of the top two corners of the camera. Tie yarn through the holes.

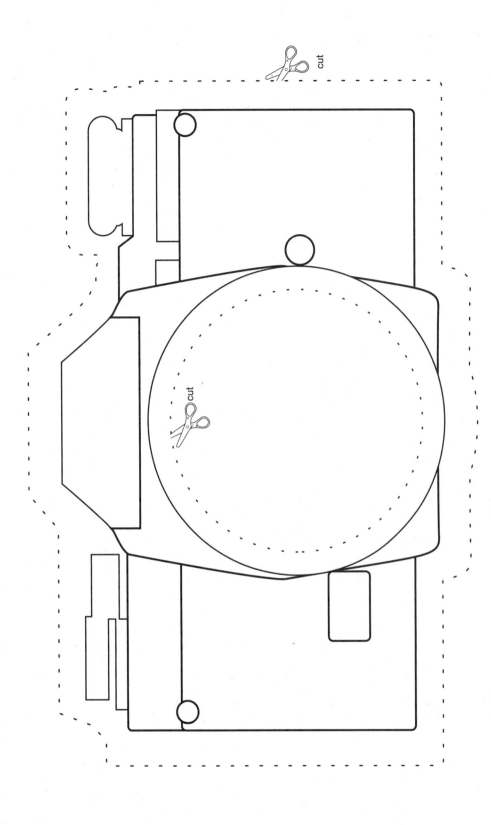

Name   Date

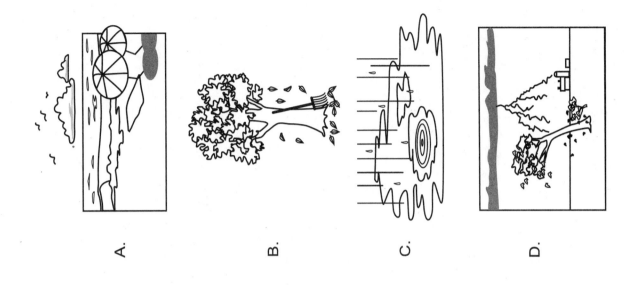

A.   B.   C.   D.

Clouds and Weather

Draw a line to match the clouds with the weather.

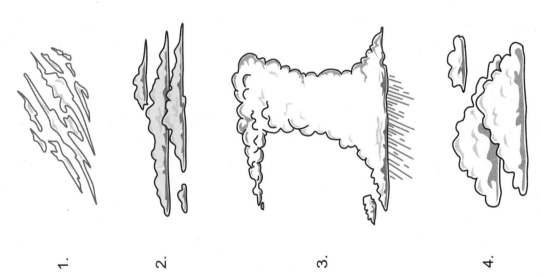

1.   2.   3.   4.

Lesson Assessment

Watching the Clouds Go By

Questions:

1. What are clouds made of?

2. What makes clouds move?

3. Are all clouds the same size and shape?

4. Which picture shows that a storm is coming?

Student Guide
Lesson 5: Raindrops and Rainbows

Lesson Objectives

- Explain that rain is water that falls from clouds in the sky.
- State that rainbows sometimes form after it rains.
- Know that rainbows are made up of red, orange, yellow, green, blue, indigo, and purple

PREPARE

Approximate lesson time is 45 minutes.

Materials

For the Student

   📖 My Weather Chart

     cotton balls

     pencils, no. 2

     pipette, plastic

     plates, paper

     glass, drinking - containing water

     paper, wax

     toothpicks

     cup, paper

     mirror, single

     bowl - clear glass

     brush, watercolor

     paints, watercolor, 8 colors or more

     paper, 8 1/2" x 11"

     water - enough to fill a bowl

Optional

     flashlight

     household items - garden hose

     cleaning items - dishwashing liquid

     sugar

     bowl

     measuring cup

     pipe cleaners

     water

Keywords and Pronunciation

rain : Water that falls from clouds. The falling rain made everyone wet.

rainbow : Colors caused by sunlight shining through water droplets. After the rain stopped, we saw a beautiful rainbow.

LEARN
Activity 1: Weather Observations *(Online)*

Activity 2: Rain *(Online)*

Activity 3: Rainbows *(Online)*

Activity 4. Optional: Rain Makes Rainbows *(Online)*

ASSESS
Lesson Assessment: Raindrops and Rainbows (*Online*)

You will complete an offline assessment covering the main objectives of this lesson. Your learning coach will score this assessment.

LEARN
Activity 5. Optional: Bubbles of Rainbows *(Online)*

My Weather Chart

Cut

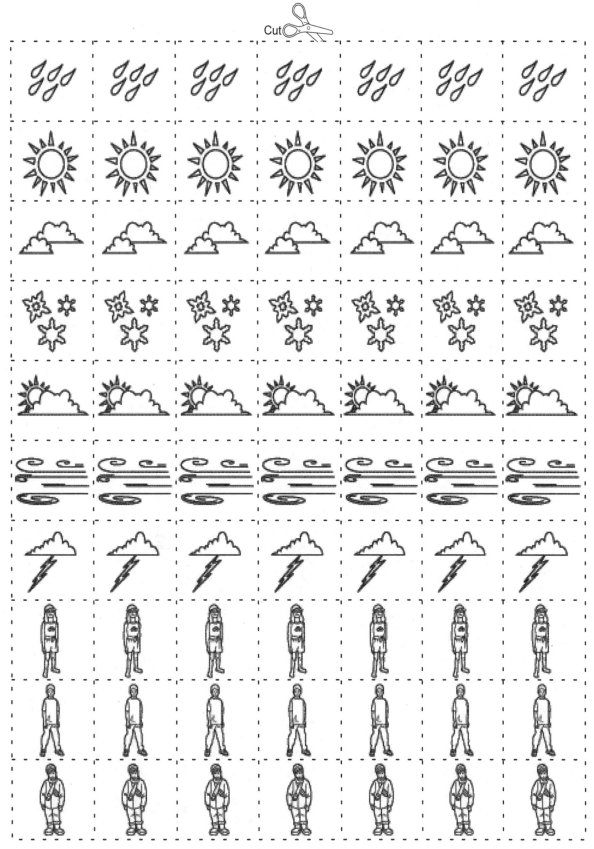

45

<u>Name</u>_____   Date_____

My Weather Chart

Day_____Date_____   Day_____Date_____

weather	temperature

weather	temperature

Day_____Date_____   Day_____Date_____

weather	temperature

weather	temperature

Day_____Date_____   Day_____Date_____

weather	temperature

weather	temperature

Lesson Assessment

Raindrops and Rainbows

Questions:

1. When water falls from a cloud, what is it called?

2. If the sun is out and it is still raining, what colorful thing might you see in the sky?

3. Name some of the colors that are in a rainbow.

Student Guide
Lesson 6: Weather Watch

Lesson Objectives

- Graph observations from a weather chart.
- Describe four types of severe weather: droughts, floods, hurricanes, and tornadoes.

PREPARE

Approximate lesson time is 45 minutes.

Materials

For the Student

   📖 My Weather Chart

   📖 My Weather Graph

   cooking equipment - tin pie pan

   map, U.S.

   household items - pitcher

   water

Optional

   bottle, plastic - 2 liter (2)

   cleaning items - dishwashing detergent

   food coloring

Keywords and Pronunciation

drought (drowt) : A long period without rain. After the long drought, the harvest did not yield many crops.

flood : Large amounts of water from rain that cause rivers to overflow their banks. Water from the flood rose as high as the bridge over the river.

hurricane : A storm with high winds and heavy rain. In a hurricane, people should leave their homes in case they are in danger of being destroyed.

tornado : Strong, funnel-shaped winds. Some tornadoes are so strong that they can lift homes and cars.

LEARN
Activity 1: Weather Observations *(Online)*

Activity 2: Graphing the Weather *(Online)*

Activity 3: Severe Weather (*Online*)

Activity 4. Optional: What Am I? (*Online*)

ASSESS

Lesson Assessment: Weather Watch (*Online*)

You will complete an offline assessment covering the main objectives of this lesson. Your learning coach will score this assessment.

LEARN

Activity 5. Optional: Make a Family Disaster Plan (*Online*)

Activity 6. Optional: Tornado in a Bottle (*Online*)

My Weather Chart

Cut

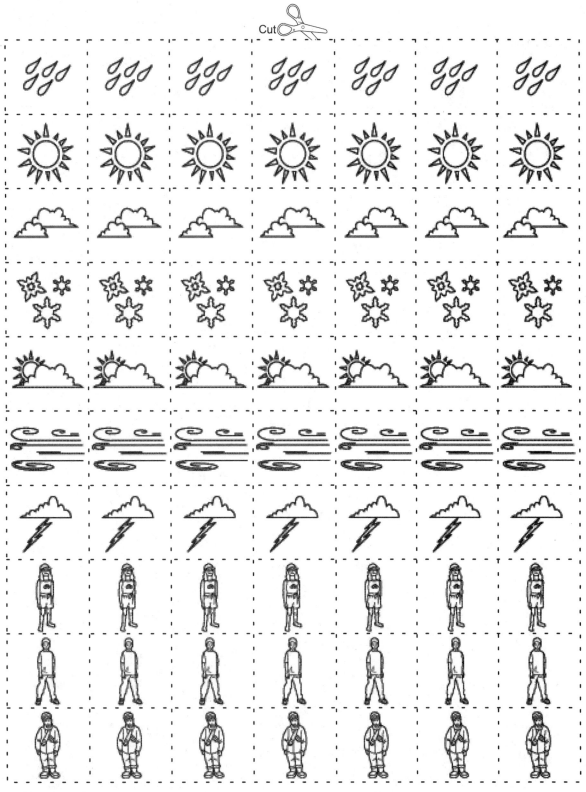

Name _____   Date _____

My Weather Chart

Day_____Date_____

weather	temperature

Day_____Date_____

weather	temperature

Day_____Date_____

weather	temperature

Day_____Date_____

weather	temperature

Day_____Date_____

weather	temperature

Day_____Date_____

weather	temperature

Name _____   Date _____

My Weather Graph

10									
9									
8									
7									
6									
5									
4									
3									
2									
1									

Lesson Assessment

Weather Watch

Questions:

1. What type of severe weather has strong funnel-shaped winds?

2. Hurricanes are storms that have strong winds and a lot of _____?

3. During a drought, what has not happened for a very long time?

4. Which picture shows a flood?

A.   B.   C.

Student Guide
Lesson 1: Falling for Fall

Discover how plants and animals change during each season and prepare for the one ahead. Follow one entire cycle of seasons, observing the changes in deciduous trees and gray squirrels. Find out how animals use a variety of methods to survive cold winters.

Lesson Objectives

- Explain that some animals gather and store food during the fall.
- Explain that the weather gets cooler in the fall.
- Recognize the changes that occur to deciduous trees in the fall.

PREPARE

Approximate lesson time is 45 minutes.

Advance Preparation

- Create paper leaves to help your student investigate the way some trees change in the fall season.
- 1. Print the Leaf Patterns sheet.
- 2. Trace the patterns on brown, yellow, orange, and red construction paper.
- 3. Cut out about 20 leaves.
- Or, if you wish, you can collect real leaves and substitute them for the paper leaves.
- In the optional review activity, your student will begin to make a seasons mural. Choose a wall where he can tape up a long piece of paper, such as butcher paper. He can add pictures to his mural throughout the unit.

Materials

For the Student
- Leaf Patterns
  food - peanuts (10)
  paper, colored construction, 12"x12" - brown, orange, yellow, red (2)
  scissors, round-end safety

Optional
  leaves
- Gray Squirrel Coloring Sheet
  crayons, 16 or more
  tape, clear
  paper, drawing, 12" x 18" (3)
  book - Autumn, Fall

Keywords and Pronunciation

deciduous (dih-SIH-juh-wuhs) : Having leaves that fall off during certain seasons or at a certain developmental stages. In the fall we rake up the leaves from deciduous trees.

evergreen : Having leaves that remain green all through the year, regardless of weather. An evergreen tree keeps its leaves all year long.

LEARN
Activity 1: Four Seasons *(Online)*

Activity 2: What Happens in the Fall? *(Online)*
Safety

This lesson involves eating or working with food. Before beginning, check with your doctor, if necessary, to find out whether your student will have any allergic reaction to the food.

Activity 3. Optional: Fall Scene *(Online)*

ASSESS

Lesson Assessment: Falling for Fall (*Online*)

You will complete an offline assessment covering the main objectives of this lesson. Your learning coach will score this assessment.

LEARN
Activity 4. Optional: Fall Month Activities *(Online)*

Activity 5. Optional: Read a Book! *(Online)*

Name _____   Date _____

Leaf Patterns

cut

Gray Squirrel Coloring Sheet

Gray Squirrel Coloring Sheet

cut

cut

Name _____ Date _____

Lesson Assessment

Falling for Fall

Questions:

1. Which picture shows a deciduous tree in fall?

A.   B.

2. How does the weather change in the fall? Does it get warmer or cooler?

3. Name something a squirrel might do in the fall to get ready for winter.

Student Guide
Lesson 2: Winter Wonderland

Lesson Objectives

- Explain that the weather is coldest in the winter.
- Recognize the changes that can occur to deciduous trees in the winter.
- Explain that food can be hard for animals to find in the winter.

PREPARE

Approximate lesson time is 45 minutes.

Materials

For the Student

⊟ Snowflake Patterns

paper, 8 1/2" x 11" (5)

scissors, round-end safety

Optional

glitter

crayons, 16 or more

tape, clear

⊟ Gray Squirrel Coloring Sheet

paper, drawing, 12" x 18" (3)

"Winter" by Maria Rius

LEARN
Activity 1: What Is Winter? *(Online)*

Activity 2: Winter Snowflakes, Winter Nuts *(Online)*
Safety

This lesson involves eating or working with food. Before beginning, check with your doctor, if necessary, to find out whether your student will have allergic reaction to the food.

Activity 3. Optional: Winter Scene *(Online)*

ASSESS

Lesson Assessment: Winter Wonderland (*Online*)

You will complete an offline assessment covering the main objectives of this lesson. Your learning coach will score this assessment.

LEARN

Activity 4. Optional: Winter Months Activities *(Online)*

Activity 5. Optional: Read a Book *(Online)*

Name _____   Date _____

Snowflake Pattern

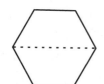

Step 1

Fold each cut hexagon in half. Line up the halves evenly.

Step 2

Fold each half into thirds, as shown.

Step 3

Now cut shapes into each folded triangle. For each snowflake, cut different shapes.

 Cut

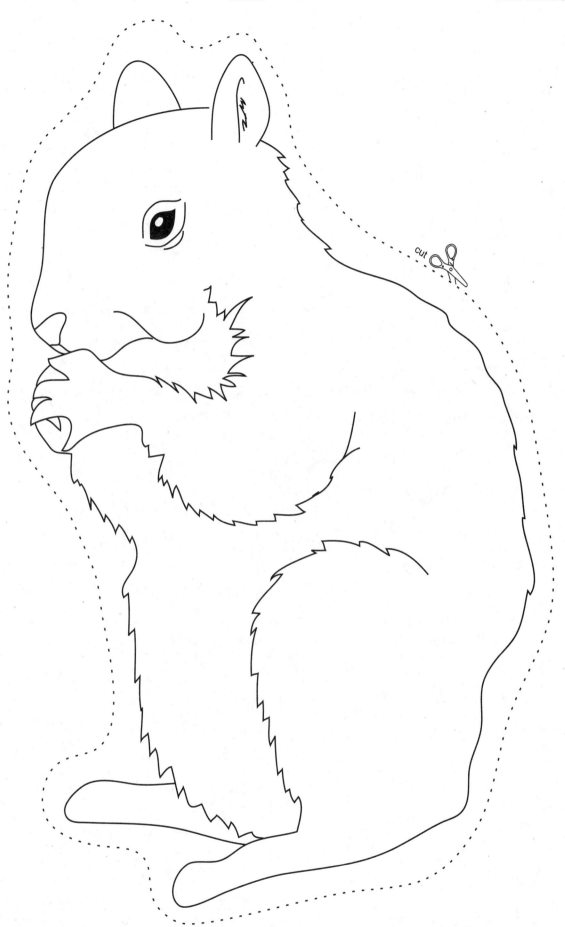

Gray Squirrel Coloring Sheet

cut

75

cut

cut

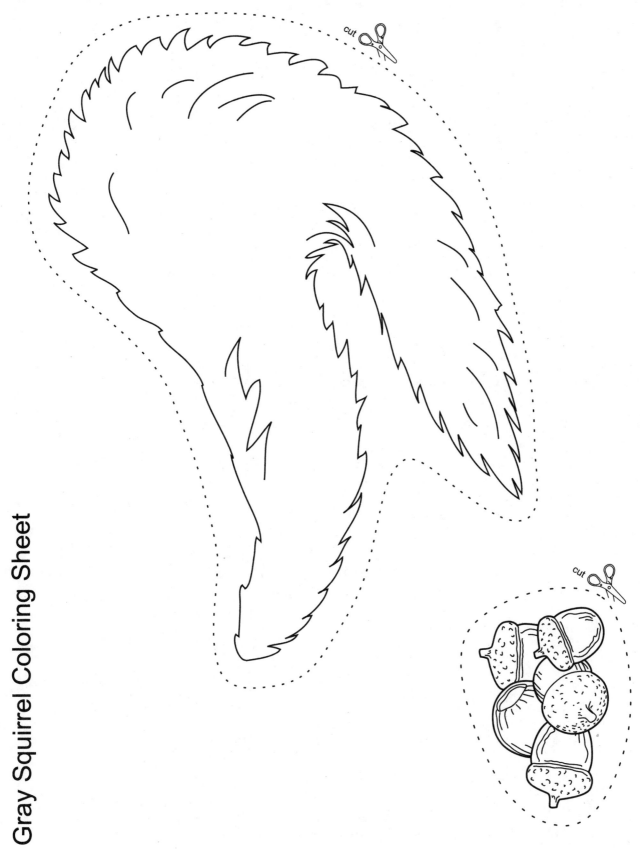

Gray Squirrel Coloring Sheet

Lesson Assessment

Winter Wonderland

Questions:

1. Which is the coldest season?

2. Which picture shows a deciduous tree in winter?

A.   B.

3. What can cover the ground in the very cold winter, making it hard for some animals to find food?

Student Guide
Lesson 3: Animals in Winter

Lesson Objectives

- Recognize that animals use different strategies to make it through cold winters (for example, hibernating, migrating, storing food, or actively searching for food and shelter.)

PREPARE

Approximate lesson time is 45 minutes.

Materials

For the Student

"Animals in Winter" by Henrietta Bancroft and Richard G. Van Gelder (ISBN 0-06-445165-8)

jugs, milk - 1 gallon

household items - birdseed

scissors, round-end safety

string

candy - gummy bear

food - chocolate syrup and creamy peanut butter

plates, paper

miniature marshmallows (4)

spoon - tablespoon

Optional

book - Backyard Birds of Winter

Keywords and Pronunciation

hibernate : To spend the winter in a deep sleep. A woodchuck crawls into its long underground tunnel and sleeps through the winter.

migrate : To move to a different place, usually at certain times or seasons. Many birds migrate south for the winter.

LEARN
Activity 1: Winter and Animals *(Online)*

Activity 2: Animals in Winter *(Online)*

Activity 3: Make a Bird Feeder *(Online)*

ASSESS

Lesson Assessment: Animals in Winter (*Online*)

You will complete an offline assessment covering the main objectives of this lesson. Your learning coach will score this assessment.

LEARN

Activity 4. Optional: Woodchuck Home *(Online)*

Safety

This lesson involves eating or working with food. Before beginning, check with your doctor, if necessary, to find out whether your student will have any allergic reaction to the food.

Activity 5. Optional: More on Birds in Winter *(Online)*

Name _____ Date _____

Lesson Assessment

Animals in Winter

Questions:

1. When animals hibernate, what are they doing? Are they moving to where it is warm or sleeping all winter long?

2. **Turn to page 16 of *Animals in Winter* and read the following to your student:**
   What is the pika gathering to eat under the snow?

3. **Turn to page 26 of *Animals in Winter* and read the following to your student:**
   How is the rabbit in this picture searching for food?

4. When birds move to warmer places for the winter, are they *migrating* or *hibernating*?

5. Name an animal that migrates south in the winter.

Student Guide
Lesson 4: Spring Has Sprung

Lesson Objectives

- Explain that the weather becomes warmer in spring.
- Explain that many animals become more active and have babies in the spring.
- Recognize the changes that occur to deciduous trees in the spring.

PREPARE

Approximate lesson time is 45 minutes.

Materials

For the Student

      📇 Leaf Patterns

      📇 Spring Flower Coloring Sheet

      bag, brown paper, lunch

      crayons, 16 or more

      paper, colored construction, 12"x12" - green (2)

      Elmer's Glue-All

      scissors, round-end safety

      📇 Gray Squirrel Coloring Sheet

      tape, clear

Optional

      paper, drawing, 12" x 18" (3)

      "Spring" by Maria Rius

LEARN
Activity 1: Spring *(Online)*

Activity 2: Flowers and Nests *(Online)*

Activity 3. Optional: Squirrel Spring *(Online)*

ASSESS
Lesson Assessment: Spring Has Sprung (*Online*)

You will complete an offline assessment covering the main objectives of this lesson. Your learning coach will score this assessment.

LEARN
Activity 4. Optional: Spring Months Activities *(Online)*

Activity 5. Optional: Read a Book *(Online)*

Name _____   Date _____

Leaf Patterns

Name _____   Date _____

Spring Flower Coloring Sheet

91

cut

Gray Squirrel Coloring Sheet

Gray Squirrel Coloring Sheet

Name _____   Date _____

Lesson Assessment

Spring Has Sprung

Questions:

1. In the spring, does the weather start to get warmer or cooler?

2. Why do some people wait until spring to plant flowers?

3. Which picture shows a deciduous tree in the middle of spring?

A.

B.

4. Name something an animal might do in the spring.

Student Guide
Lesson 5: Summer Sun

Lesson Objectives

- Explain that the weather is warmest in the summer.
- Explain that the seasons continuously cycle from one to the next, always in the same order.
- Recognize the changes that occur in many deciduous trees in the summer.

PREPARE

Approximate lesson time is 45 minutes.

Materials

For the Student

    📖 Seasons Go 'Round

    crayons, 16 or more

    pencils, no. 2

    can, tin - coffee

    tape, clear

    📖 Gray Squirrel Coloring Sheet

    paper, colored construction, 12"x12" - green

    scissors, round-end safety

Optional

    Elmer's Glue-All

    paper, drawing, 12" x 18" (3)

    "Summer" by Maria Rius

LEARN
Activity 1: Summer *(Online)*

Activity 2: Summer into Fall Again *(Online)*

Activity 3. Optional: Seasons Change *(Online)*

ASSESS

Lesson Assessment: Summer Sun (*Online*)

You will complete an offline assessment covering the main objectives of this lesson. Your learning coach will score this assessment.

LEARN

Activity 4. Optional: Make a Calendar (*Online*)

Activity 5. Optional: Read a Book (*Online*)

Name _____   Date _____

Seasons Going 'Round

Gray Squirrel Coloring Sheet

cut

cut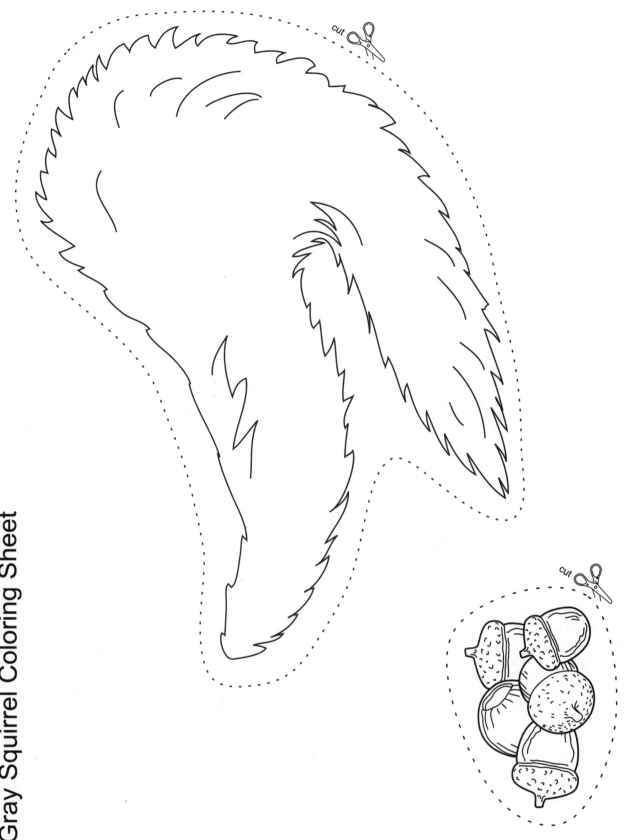

Gray Squirrel Coloring Sheet

cut

Name _____   Date _____

Lesson Assessment

Summer Sun

Questions:

1. Which picture shows a deciduous tree in summer?

A.   B.

2. Which of these could someone do outdoors in the average summer--swim in a pool or make a snowman?

3. Which season is the warmest?

4. What season comes next--fall, winter, spring, summer, _____.

5. Do the seasons always happen in the same order?

Student Guide
Lesson 1: The Shape of the Earth

Get to know some of the major physical features of our planet, the Earth. Learn that the Earth is spherical in shape. Build a model showing common land shapes and bodies of water found on the Earth's surface.

Lesson Objectives
- Define Earth as the name of our world.
- Identify the shape of the Earth as a sphere.
- Locate the North Pole, South Pole, and the equator on a globe.

PREPARE

Approximate lesson time is 45 minutes.

Advance Preparation
- For this science lesson you will need to gather some items that are spherical and some that are circular. Spherical objects may include a tennis ball, a golf ball, a balloon, or an orange. Circular objects may include coins, a plate, a cookie, or a wall clock.

Materials
For the Student
    ball, rubber
    clock - round
    food - round cookie
    plates, paper
    ball - tennis
    balloon
    coins
    fruits - round
    📖 Map of Earth Outline
    globe, inflatable
    tacks (2)
    map, world
    scissors, round-end safety
    tape, clear
Optional
    crayons, 16 or more
    📖 The Shape of the Earth Review

Keywords and Pronunciation

Earth : The planet on which we live. The Earth is home to plants and animals.

equator : An imaginary line drawn around the middle of the Earth. The equator is located halfway between the North and South Poles.

globe : A model of the Earth that shows its shape. You can look at a globe to see what the whole Earth looks like.

North Pole : The northernmost point on the Earth, located at the top of a globe. Can you find the North Pole on the globe?

South Pole : The southernmost point on the Earth, located at the bottom of a globe. The South Pole is directly opposite the North Pole.

sphere : Something round, like a ball. The Earth is shaped like a ball; both are spheres.

LEARN
Activity 1: Where Do You Live? *(Online)*

Activity 2: The Earth Is a Sphere *(Online)*

Activity 3: Where's the North Pole? *(Online)*

Activity 4. Optional: The Shape of the Earth Review *(Online)*

ASSESS

Lesson Assessment: The Shape of the Earth (*Online*)

You will complete an offline assessment covering the main objectives of this lesson. Your learning coach will score this assessment.

Map of Earth Outline

Cut out the flat map of Earth. Wrap the map around the tennis ball and place a piece of tape near the middle. Then tape down the ends.

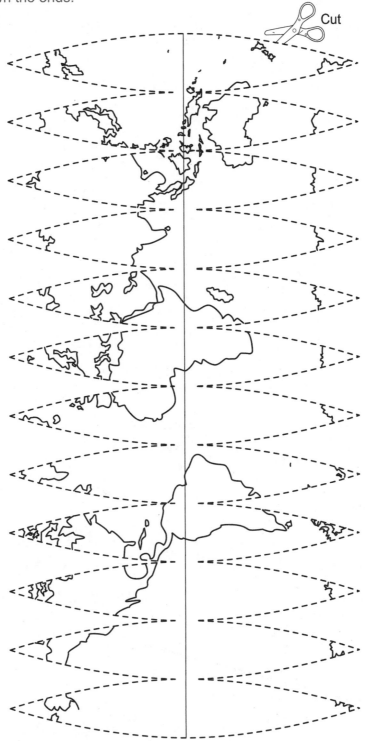

Name _____   Date _____

The Shape of the Earth Review

Circle the picture that shows where you live.

Circle the picture that shows something that is a sphere.

On the picture of planet Earth, place an 'X' over the
North Pole, circle the South Pole, and draw a line where
the equator should be.

Lesson Assessment

The Shape of the Earth

1. What is the name of the world we live on?

2. What shape is planet Earth?

3. **For this question, refer to your student's responses in the *Where's the North Pole* activity earlier in this lesson.**
   Locate the North Pole, South Pole, and the equator on a globe.

Student Guide
Lesson 2: The Earth's Surface

Lesson Objectives

- Explain that the Earth's surface is composed of land and water.
- Explain that more of the Earth's surface is covered by water than by land.
- Identify the large areas of land on Earth as continents.
- Identify the large areas of water on Earth as oceans.

PREPARE

Approximate lesson time is 45 minutes.

Materials

For the Student

    food - egg

    🖳 Land and Water, Oceans and Continents

    beans, dried - green split pea, yellow split pea, and two other varieties

    globe, inflatable

    soil - potting

    glass, drinking

    map, world

    rocks

    water

Optional

    paper - sticky label

    crayons, 16 or more

    scissors, round-end safety

Keywords and Pronunciation

continent : A large area of land on Earth. There are seven continents on the planet Earth.

ocean : A large area of water on Earth. Sharks and whales swim in the ocean.

surface : The outside layer of something. The surface of the table is smooth and hard.

LEARN
Activity 1: What Is a Surface? *(Online)*

Activity 2: Land and Water, Oceans and Continents *(Online)*

Activity 3. Optional: Continents and Oceans Puzzle *(Online)*

ASSESS

Lesson Assessment: The Earth's Surface (*Online*)

You will complete an offline assessment covering the main objectives of this lesson. Your learning coach will score this assessment.

LEARN

Activity 4. Optional: Name the Continents and Oceans *(Online)*

Name

Date

Land and Water, Oceans and Continents

Lesson Assessment

The Earth's Surface

1. The Earth's surface is made up of _____ and _____.

2. Does more water or more land cover the Earth's surface?

3. What are the large areas of water on Earth called?

4. What do we call the seven large areas of land on Earth?

Student Guide
Lesson 3: Land Shapes

Lesson Objectives
- Recognize that land on Earth has different shapes.
- Identify mountains, valleys, hills, islands, and plains.

PREPARE

Approximate lesson time is 45 minutes.

Materials

For the Student
- globe, inflatable
- map, world
- clay, colored - blue, yellow, green
- cookie sheet

Optional
- brochures, travel
- glue sticks
- magazines
- paper, colored construction, 12"x12"
- paper, heavy - posterboard
- scissors, round-end safety

Keywords and Pronunciation

hill : An area of land that is higher than the land around it, but not as high as a mountain. We go sledding down the hill behind my house in the winter.

island : A piece of land surrounded by water. You must take the ferryboat to reach the island.

mountain : An area of land that rises high above the land around it. It is hard to hike up most mountains because they are so high.

plain : A wide stretch of flat land. Buffaloes used to roam the plains.

valley : A low area of land, usually surrounded by hills or mountains. Valleys often have a river or stream running through them.

LEARN
Activity 1: The Shape of Your Neighbhorhood *(Online)*

Activity 2: The Shape of the Land *(Online)*
Safety
Use nontoxic clay for the activity.

Activity 3. Optional: Review Landshapes *(Online)*

ASSESS
Lesson Assessment: Land Shapes (*Online*)
You will complete an offline assessment covering the main objectives of this lesson. Your learning coach will score this assessment.

LEARN
Activity 4. Optional: Land Shapes Collage *(Online)*

Lesson Assessment

Land Shapes

1. Which is smaller, a mountain or a hill?

2. What is the name of a low area of land between higher areas of land--a valley or plain?

3. What do you call a piece of land surrounded by water?

Student Guide
Lesson 4: Bodies of Water

Lesson Objectives

- Identify oceans, lakes, ponds, rivers, and streams as bodies of water on the surface of the Earth.

PREPARE

Approximate lesson time is 45 minutes.

Materials

For the Student

      globe, inflatable

      map, world

      clay, colored - blue

Optional

      scissors, round-end safety

      yarn - blue

      pebbles

      soil

      twigs

Keywords and Pronunciation

lake : A large body of water, generally wider and deeper than a pond. Some lakes are so large you can ski across them behind a motorboat.

ocean : The largest body of water on the surface of the Earth. The Earth has four main oceans. It takes a long time to sail across the ocean.

pond : A body of water generally smaller and shallower than a lake. You can often find frogs near the edge of a small pond.

river : A large, long body of water that flows around bends and empties into another river, a lake, or an ocean. You can canoe down a river.

stream : A small body of water, narrower and usually shorter than a river, that flows into other streams, rivers, lakes, ponds, or even into oceans. Sometimes you can hop from rock to rock across a narrow stream.

LEARN
Activity 1: What About the Water? (Online)

Activity 2: What Type of Body of Water? *(Online)*

Activity 3. Optional: Different Bodies of Water *(Online)*

ASSESS

Lesson Assessment: Bodies of Water (*Online*)

You will complete an offline assessment covering the main objectives of this lesson. Your learning coach will score this assessment.

LEARN

Activity 4. Optional: Finishing Touches *(Online)*

Lesson Assessment

Bodies of Water

1. Which is wider--a stream or a river?

2. Which is bigger--a lake or a pond?

3. Name the biggest body of water on the Earth.

Student Guide
Lesson 5: Rocks and Soil

129

Lesson Objectives

- Explain that land is made of rocks and soil, and that rocks are found all over the Earth, even under bodies of water.
- Sort rocks by size and by texture.
- Explain that soil is made of tiny bits of rock mixed with other bits of things like leaves, worms, and bugs, living and dead.

PREPARE

Approximate lesson time is 45 minutes.

Advance Preparation

- For this science lesson, your student will need approximately 6-12 small rocks and a small soil sample. If possible, help your student collect a variety of rocks from different locations. This can be done before or during the lesson.

- Spread out newspaper over a convenient surface where your student can look at his rocks and soil.

Materials

For the Student
    globe, inflatable
    plastic sandwich bags, zipper-closed (2)
    soil - 2-3 Tbsp.
    magnifying glass
    newspaper - or magazines
    rocks (10)
    shovel

Optional
    crayons, 16 or more
    paper, drawing, 12" x 18"
    "I am a Rock" by Jean Marzollo
    "If You Find a Rock" by Peggy Christian
    grass - dried
    soil
    household items - ice-cube trays
    water

Keywords and Pronunciation

rock : What land is made of; rocks can be as small as a grain of sand or as big as a mountain. Many old buildings, such as the Pyramids in Egypt, are made of rock.

soil : Tiny bits of rock mixed with other bits of things like leaves, worms, and bugs, living and dead. John used a shovel to dig a hole in the soil.

LEARN
Activity 1: Rocks All Over *(Online)*

Activity 2: A Closer Look *(Online)*

Activity 3. Optional: Rocks and Soil Picture *(Online)*

ASSESS

Lesson Assessment: Rocks and Soil (*Online*)

You will complete an offline assessment covering the main objectives of this lesson. Your learning coach will score this assessment.

LEARN
Activity 4. Optional: Reading Further *(Online)*

Activity 5. Optional: Rock Structures *(Online)*

Activity 6. Optional: Make a Brick Building *(Online)*

Lesson Assessment

Rocks and Soil

1. What two things make up the land on the Earth?

2. Are there rocks at the bottom of the ocean?

3. Yes or No: Both small rocks and dead leaves can be found in soil.

4. **For this question, refer to your student's responses in the *A Closer Look* activity earlier in this lesson.**
   Place the rocks in two groups: large and small. Now place the rocks in two groups: rough and smooth.

Student Guide
Lesson 1: The Earth Gives Us So Much

Learn about how much the Earth gives us--and how we have to be responsible for not polluting our planet. Discover some things you can do to help conserve water, trees, and electricity. Finally, meet Rachel Carson, a world-famous conservationist who showed us how closely connected we are to nature.

Lesson Objectives

- Identify water and trees as resources we use every day.

PREPARE

Approximate lesson time is 45 minutes.

Advance Preparation

- If you plan on making paper in this science lesson you may wish to prepare ahead of time by building a paper-making screen. To do so, attach a piece of window screen to an old picture frame with small nails or staples.

Materials

For the Student
> pencils, no. 2
> paper, 8 1/2" x 11"
> 🖥 Water, Water Everywhere

Optional
> blender
> cooking equipment - spatula
> rolling pin
> sieve
> household items - towel
> newspaper - or magazines
> paper - white

LEARN

Activity 1: The Earth Gives Us What We Need *(Online)*

Activity 2: Trees *(Online)*

Activity 3: Water *(Online)*

Activity 4. Optional: What the Earth Gave Me Today *(Online)*

ASSESS
Lesson Assessment: The Earth Gives Us So Much (*Online*)
You will complete an offline assessment covering the main objectives of this lesson. Your learning coach will score this assessment.

LEARN
Activity 5. Optional: Making Paper *(Online)*

Name _____ Date _____

Water, Water Everywhere!

Circle all the ways that you use water.

Name _____   Date _____

Lesson Assessment

The Earth Gives Us So Much

1. Name two things you use that are made from trees.

2. Name one way people use water to have fun.

3. **For this question, refer to your student's responses during your "wood walk" in the *Trees* activity earlier in this lesson.**
   How many wooden things can you find around your home? Make a picture of anything you see that is made of wood.

4. **For this question, refer to your student's responses during your "water walk" in the *Water* activity earlier in this lesson.**
   Can you identify the way water is used around the home? Point out examples as you find them: sinks, toilets, ice cubes, sponges, mops and buckets (for cleaning), dishwasher, washing machine, and so on.

Student Guide
Lesson 2: Why Should We Conserve?

Lesson Objectives
- State one way to conserve water and one way to conserve electricity.

PREPARE

Approximate lesson time is 45 minutes.

Advance Preparation
- Before beginning this lesson, turn on a few lights and a radio in different rooms that are not being used. Turn on a water faucet in a bathroom to a very slow drip.
- If you plan to do the Extension for this lesson, you will need to locate the electric meter for your home or building.

Materials
For the Student
> toothpaste
>
> bowl - large
>
> cup
>
> toothbrush

Optional
> 🖥 Conservers and Wasters

Keywords and Pronunciation
conserve : To use only what you need and not to waste something. To conserve water, turn off the faucet when you brush your teeth.

reduce : To use less of something or to waste less. Write on both sides of a piece of paper to reduce the amount of paper you use.

LEARN
Activity 1: Why Conserve? *(Online)*

Activity 2: Conservation Scavenger Hunt *(Online)*

Activity 3. Optional: Conservers and Wasters (Online)

ASSESS

Lesson Assessment: Why Should We Conserve? (Online)

You will complete an offline assessment covering the main objectives of this lesson. Your learning coach will score this assessment.

LEARN

Activity 4. Optional: Shower or Bath? (Online)

Activity 5. Optional: Reading the Meter (Online)

Name _____   Date _____

Conservers and Wasters

Circle the 'C' or 'W' in each picture to tell whether the children are conserving or wasting.

Lesson Assessment

Why Should We Conserve?

1. Which picture shows someone conserving water?

A.

B.

2. Which picture shows someone conserving electricity?

A.

B.

3. Name one way you can conserve water.

4. Name one way you can conserve electricity.

Student Guide
Lesson 3: Is There a Solution to Pollution?

Lesson Objectives
- Describe different ways to keep the Earth clean.
- Identify water and land pollution.

PREPARE

Approximate lesson time is 45 minutes.

Materials

For the Student

      bowl - large

      cookie sheet

      cup

      paper, 8 1/2" x 11" - torn in pieces

      water

Optional

      drink mix, powdered

      paints, finger

      📖 Pollution or Solution?

      cleaning items - bag-plastic garbage, gloves-rubber

      cleaning items - paper towel

      mug, ceramic - heat-proof

      candle, votive

      matches

Keywords and Pronunciation

pollution : Trash and other harmful things that damage or dirty the air, water, or land. The pollution thrown in the pond made it unsafe for swimming.

LEARN
Activity 1: Keep It Clean *(Online)*

Activity 2: Why Should We Keep It Clean? *(Online)*

Activity 3. Optional: Pollution or Solution? *(Online)*

ASSESS

Lesson Assessment: Is There a Solution to Pollution? (*Online*)

You will complete an offline assessment covering the main objectives of this lesson. Your learning coach will score this assessment.

LEARN

Activity 4. Optional: Trash Walk *(Online)*

Safety

When picking up trash, be mindful of broken glass or other sharp objects that may cut your student.

Activity 5. Optional: Air Can Be Polluted, Too! *(Online)*

Safety

Be careful around open flame. Do not hold the mug in the flame for more than a few seconds at a time, as the mug may become too hot to touch. Always keep the flame away from hair, clothing, and other flammable items.

Name _____ Date _____

Pollution or Solution?

Draw a smiley face under the pictures that show someone who is helping keep the Earth clean. Draw a sad face under the pictures that show pollution.

1. ○

2. ○

3. ○

4. ○

Lesson Assessment

Is There a Solution to Pollution?

1. **For this question, ask your student to look at the *Pollution or Solution?* worksheet.**
   Which picture shows water being polluted?

2. **For this question, ask your student to look at the *Pollution or Solution?* worksheet.**
   Which picture shows land being polluted?

3. Name one thing you will do today to help keep the Earth clean.

Name _____   **Date** _____

Pollution or Solution?

Draw a smiley face under the pictures that show someone who is helping keep the Earth clean. Draw a sad face under the pictures that show pollution.

Student Guide
Lesson 4: Reduce, Reuse, Recycle

Lesson Objectives

- State that one way to conserve is to reduce the amount of paper you throw away.

PREPARE

Approximate lesson time is 45 minutes.

Advance Preparation

- In this science lesson your student will be sorting paper trash. You will need to selectively save some trash such as paper plates, juice boxes, toilet paper/paper towel tubes, newspaper, junk mail, cereal boxes, packaging, paper bags, napkins, cardboard boxes, magazines and catalogs, or phone books. For the purposes of the lesson, include items that can be reused or recycled, or items you could use less often. Do not save anything you do not want your student to handle.

- Visit the Earth's 911 website to find out what paper items are recycled in your area. Click the Resources tab on the Lesson Overview screen for a link to this site.

Materials

For the Student

    cleaning items - rubber gloves

    household items - collected trash, trash bag

Optional

    crayons, 16 or more

    paper, drawing, 12" x 18"

    "Follow that Trash! All About Recycling" by Francine Jacobs

Keywords and Pronunciation

conserve : To use only what you need and not to waste something. To conserve water, turn off the faucet when you brush your teeth.

recycle : To change trash or waste into something we can use. We recycle plastic bottles to make other things, such as playground equipment or park benches.

LEARN
Activity 1: Use Less! *(Online)*

Activity 2: Sorting Trash *(Online)*
Safety
You may want to have your student wear rubber gloves while he sorts the trash.

Activity 3. Optional: How Are They Helping? *(Online)*

ASSESS
Lesson Assessment: Reduce, Reuse, Recycle (*Online*)
You will complete an offline assessment covering the main objectives of this lesson. Your learning coach will score this assessment.

LEARN
Activity 4. Optional: Read About Recycling *(Online)*

Activity 5. Optional: Recycle the Rest! *(Online)*
Safety
Use care when handling glass and metal containers. Tell your student that metal cans may have sharp lids.

Lesson Assessment

Reduce, Reuse, Recycle

1. What is one thing you can do to reduce the amount of paper you throw away?

Student Guide
Lesson 5: Biography: Rachel Carson

Lesson Objectives

- Tell that Rachel Carson studied and wrote books about nature.
- Observe and record things found in nature.

PREPARE

Approximate lesson time is 45 minutes.

Materials

For the Student

3-hole punch

crayons, 16 or more

magnifying glass

paper, 8 1/2" x 11" - 2 colored construction, 5 regular (7)

yarn

Optional

camera

clipboard

ribbon

Keywords and Pronunciation

nature : Everything that is not made by people. Trees, flowers, and birds are part of nature, but cars, houses, and forks are not.

LEARN
Activity 1: Rachel Carson: Conservationist *(Online)*

Activity 2: Nature Book *(Online)*

ASSESS

Lesson Assessment: Biography: Rachel Carson (*Online*)

You will complete an offline assessment covering the main objectives of this lesson. Your learning coach will score this assessment.

LEARN
Activity 3. Optional: Earth Day *(Online)*

Activity 4. Optional: Further Reading *(Online)*

Activity 5. Optional: U.S. EPA's Explorer's Club *(Online)*

Lesson Assessment

Biography: Rachel Carson

1. Did Rachel Carson write books about nature or about cooking?

2. **For this question, refer to your student's responses in the *Nature Book* activity earlier in this lesson.**
   Examine ten blades of grass with a magnifying glass. Make a drawing or rubbing and label it *Grass*. Find four other items from nature and repeat the process.

Student Guide
Lesson 1. Optional: Down on the Farm

This unit is OPTIONAL. It is provided for students who seek enrichment or extra practice.
Create a model farm and describe the work of a farmer such as planting and harvesting crops and milking cows. Visit four types of farms, each specializing in growing crops or raising livestock. Examine the role farms play in producing food and clothing for people.

Lesson Objectives

- Identify different types of animals that live on a farm and match animal babies with animal adults.
- Explain that farmers use land on a farm to grow crops in orchards and fields.
- Describe the role of a farmer.

PREPARE

Approximate lesson time is 45 minutes.

Advance Preparation

- For this science lesson, you may want to prepare your student by having him think about what a normal day is like for a farmer. Have him wake up early and dress in work clothes, such as overalls and boots, to get ready for his day on the farm.

Materials

For the Student
Optional
     books - with farm pictures
     🖥 My Farm
     cardboard, boxes - 12" by 18", low sides
     carton, milk - 1/2 gal., empty
     crayons, 16 or more
     food - unpopped popcorn kernels
     paper, colored construction, 12"x12"
     soil - potting
     toilet paper tubes
     plastic wrap
     popsicle sticks (10)
     scissors, adult
     scissors, round-end safety
     🖥 Animals and Their Babies
     marker, black permanent, non-toxic

Keywords and Pronunciation

crops : Plants grown on a farm. Good soil, water, and sunlight are needed to grow healthy crops.

manure : Animal waste that is spread on soil to add nutrients that help plants grow. The farmer spreads manure on the field before planting the corn.

orchard : An area of trees planted to grow food. We like to visit the apple orchard and pick apples off the trees.

LEARN
Activity 1. Optional: Optional Lesson Instructions *(Online)*

This lesson is OPTIONAL. It is provided for students who seek enrichment or extra practice. You may skip this lesson.

If you choose to skip this lesson, then go to the Plan or Lesson Lists page and mark this lesson "Skipped" in order to proceed to the next lesson in the course.

Activity 2. Optional: What's on a Farm? *(Online)*

Activity 3. Optional: My Farm *(Online)*

Activity 4. Optional: Animals and Their Babies *(Online)*

Activity 5. Optional: A Day on My Farm *(Online)*

Activity 6. Optional: Only on the Farm *(Online)*

My Farm

Color and cut out the farmer, cornfield and orchard. Glue them to craft sticks.

Cut

Cut

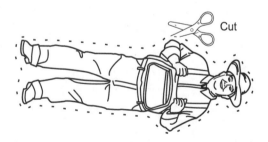

My Farm

Color and cut out the farmer, cornfield and orchard. Glue them to craft sticks.

✂ Cut

Farm Animal Babies

Sheep and _____

Horse and _____

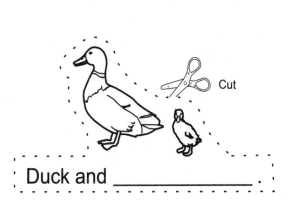

Duck and _____

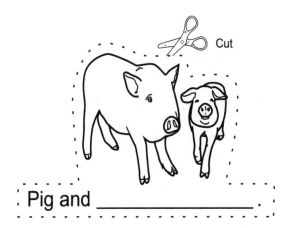

Pig and _____

Farm Animal Babies

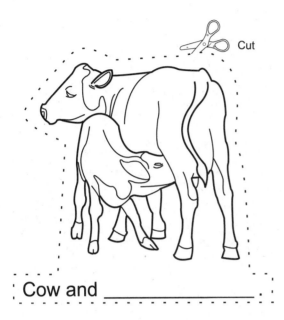

Cut

Cow and _____

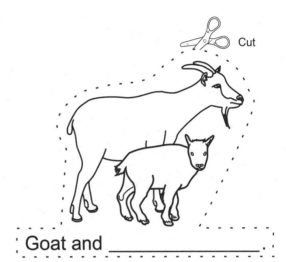

Cut

Goat and _____

Cut

Chicken and _____

Student Guide
Lesson 2. Optional: Find My Farm

Lesson Objectives
- Identify four different types of farms: poultry, dairy, wheat, and cotton.
- Match products to the farms from which they come
- Recognize that crops are plants that are grown on farms.
- Recognize that livestock is another name for animals raised farms.

PREPARE

Approximate lesson time is 45 minutes.

Advance Preparation
- In this science lesson you will need to collect a variety of items for your student to examine that are products from farms that grow wheat (bread, pasta, crackers, and cereal), dairy (milk, butter, yogurt, cheese), poultry (eggs), and cotton (shirts, socks).

Materials
  For the Student
  - Farms, Part 1
  - Farms, Part 2
      clothing - cotton
      crayons, 16 or more
      food - dairy products, egg, sliced bread
      paper, colored construction, 12"x12"
      Elmer's Glue-All
      scissors, round-end safety
      stapler
  Optional
      cotton balls
      magazines - clothing advertisements
      newspaper - or magazines - food store advertisements

Keywords and Pronunciation
crops : Plants grown on a farm. Good soil, water, and sunlight are needed to grow crops.

hay : Grass that is cut, dried, and fed to farm animals. In the winter, when snow covers the ground, the farmer feeds hay to the cows.

livestock : Animals raised on farms. A well-built barn provides shelter for livestock in bad weather.

poultry : Fowl, such as chickens or turkeys, that are raised for their meat or eggs. On the poultry farm, the farmer feeds corn to the chickens.

sow : To plant seeds in the ground. The farmer sows the wheat in the field.

udder : A bag-like organ on certain animals, such as cows or goats, containing glands that produce milk. A cow's milk is drawn from its udder by a milking machine.

LEARN
Activity 1. Optional: Optional Lesson Instructions *(Online)*

This lesson is OPTIONAL. It is provided for students who seek enrichment or extra practice. You may skip this lesson.

If you choose to skip this lesson, then go to the Plan or Lesson Lists page and mark this lesson "Skipped" in order to proceed to the next lesson in the course.

Activity 2. Optional: Crops and Livestock *(Online)*

Activity 3. Optional: Tour of Farms *(Online)*

Activity 4. Optional: It Comes from Where? *(Online)*

Activity 5. Optional: Aquaculture *(Online)*

Activity 6. Optional: Farmers Market *(Online)*

Name _____ Date _____

Farms

Name _____   Date _____

Farms

Farms

Cut out the images and glue them into the correct farm scene.

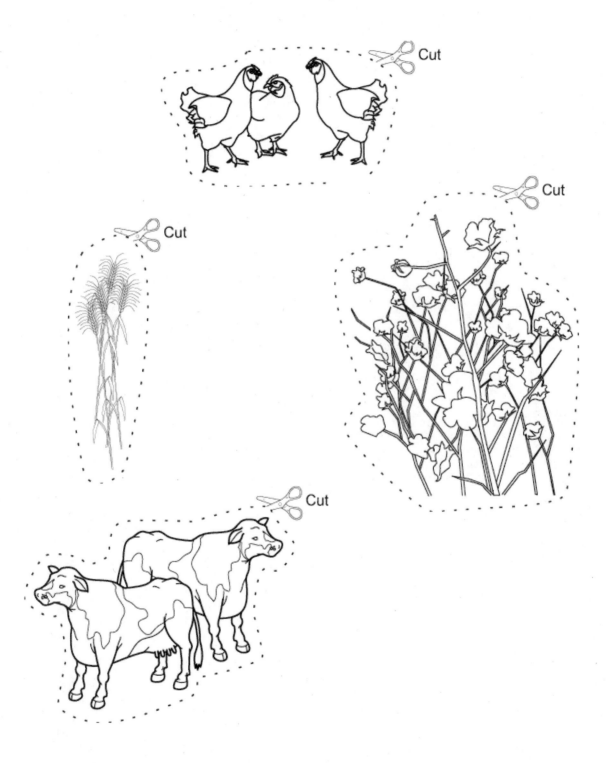

Farms

Cut out the images and glue them into the correct farm scene.

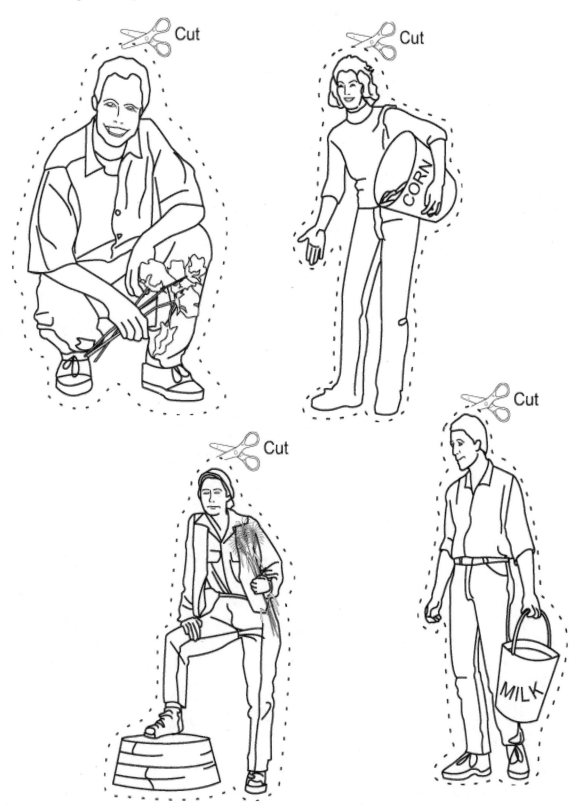

Student Guide
Lesson 3. Optional: Milking It

Lesson Objectives

- Describe the needs of cows on a dairy farm.
- Identify products that come from dairy cows.
- Describe the process of milking a dairy cow.
- Sequence the process of milk production from cow to grocery store.

PREPARE

Approximate lesson time is 45 minutes.

Advance Preparation

- Place the container you will use for making the butter into the freezer at least an hour before use. Also chill the heavy cream you plan to use--it should be extremely cold, but not frozen.

Materials

For the Student

> food - crackers, bread, heavy cream
>
> jar
>
> knife, kitchen - butter knife
>
> lid, jar
>
> salt
>
> measuring cup

Optional

> electric mixer
>
> 💻 Upsy Daisy Dairy Farm
>
> crayons, 16 or more
>
> pencils, no. 2
>
> "Milk: From Cow to Carton" by Aliki

Keywords and Pronunciation

hay : Grass that is cut, dried, and fed to farm animals. In the winter, when snow covers the ground, the farmer feeds hay to the cows.

udder : A bag-like organ on certain animals, such as cows or goats, containing glands that produce milk. A cow's milk is drawn from its udder by a milking machine.

LEARN

Activity 1. Optional: Optional Lesson Instructions *(Online)*

This lesson is OPTIONAL. It is provided for students who seek enrichment or extra practice. You may skip this lesson.

If you choose to skip this lesson, then go to the Plan or Lesson Lists page and mark this lesson "Skipped" in order to proceed to the next lesson in the course.

Activity 2. Optional: It All Starts with a Moo *(Online)*

Activity 3. Optional: Getting the Milk You Need *(Online)*

Safety

Use caution when handling the knife.

Please be aware that this lesson involves eating or using food. Before conducting the lesson, check with your doctor to assess whether your student will have any allergic reaction to this food.

Activity 4. Optional: Upsy Daisy Dairy Farm *(Online)*

Activity 5. Optional: More About Milking *(Online)*

Activity 6. Optional: Visit the Barnyard Palace *(Online)*

Date

Upsy Daisy Dairy Farm

There are five things wrong on the dairy farm. Cross out each mistake and then tell how it should be corrected.

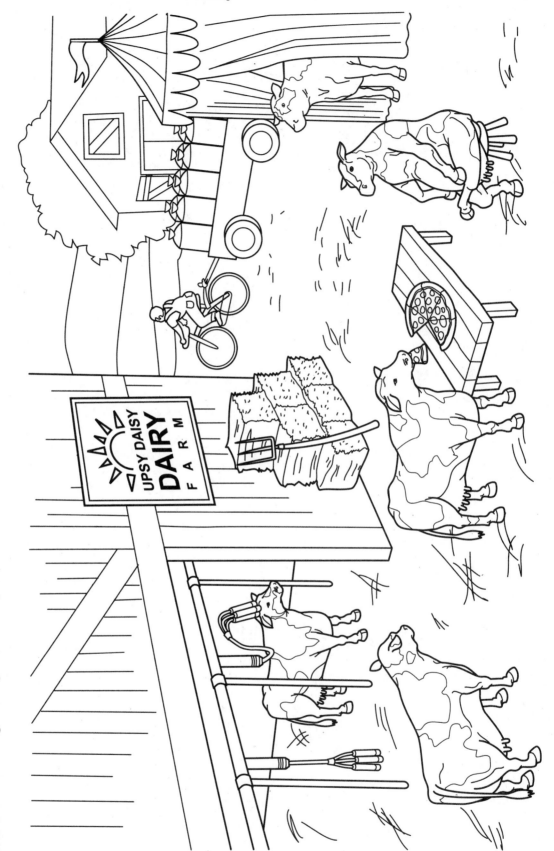

Student Guide
Lesson 4. Optional: Farms Grow Crops

Lesson Objectives

- Explain that farmers plant and care for crops.
- Identify some of the differences between caring for farm animals and caring for crops.
- Identify machines used for planting crops.

PREPARE

Approximate lesson time is 45 minutes.

Advance Preparation

- If you don't already have it, you will need corn seeds for the Planting and Plowing activity.

Materials

For the Student

    seeds, corn

    fork

Optional

    plastic sandwich bags, zipper-closed

    soil

    water

    🖳 Scarecrow Pattern

    paper, colored construction, 12"x12" - scraps

    cup

    markers, colored, 8 or more

    popsicle sticks

    scissors, round-end safety

    tape, clear

    yarn

    🖳 Seed to Crop Review

    crayons, 16 or more

    scissors, adult

    cooking equipment - oven, mixing spoon or spatula

    food - oil, cornmeal

    salt

    bowl - mixing

    cookie sheet

    labels - food (5)

    spoon - measuring

    water - boiling

Keywords and Pronunciation

manure : Animal waste that is spread on soil to add nutrients that help plants grow. The farmer spreads manure on the field before planting the corn.

LEARN
Activity 1. Optional: Optional Lesson Instructions *(Online)*

This lesson is OPTIONAL. It is provided for students who seek enrichment or extra practice. You may skip this lesson.

If you choose to skip this lesson, then go to the Plan or Lesson Lists page and mark this lesson "Skipped" in order to proceed to the next lesson in the course.

Activity 2. Optional: Crops Need Care *(Online)*

Activity 3. Optional: Planting and Plowing *(Online)*

Activity 4. Optional: Crop Care and Protection *(Online)*

Activity 5. Optional: The Planting Process *(Online)*

Activity 6. Optional: Make Corn Chips *(Online)*
Safety

Please be aware that this lesson involves eating or using food. Before conducting the lesson, check with your doctor to assess whether your student will have any allergic reaction to this food.

Activity 7. Optional: Visit a Wheat Farm *(Online)*

Scarecrow Pattern

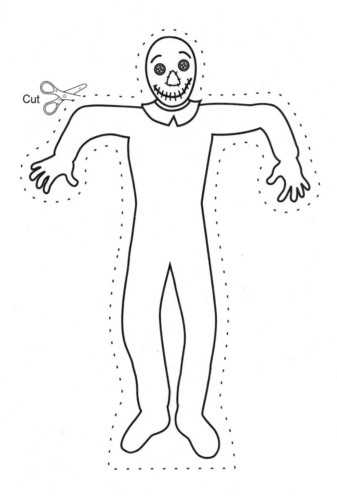

Cut

Seed to Crop Review

Cut out and place the cards in the correct order.

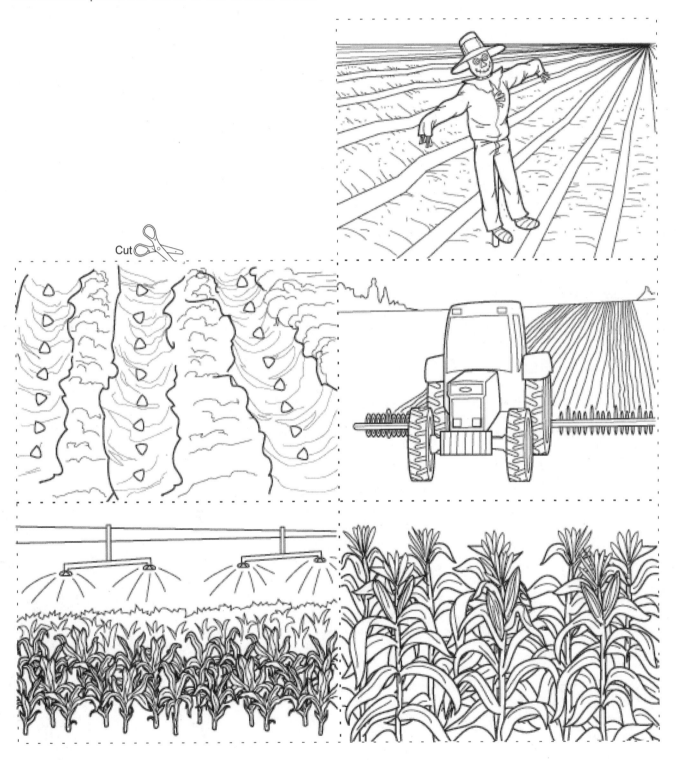

Cut

Student Guide
Lesson 5. Optional: From Crop to Table

Lesson Objectives

- Show the steps of harvesting, processing, and packaging corn.
- Explain the role farms play in everyday life.
- Use terminology to explain farm production.

PREPARE

Approximate lesson time is 45 minutes.

Materials

For the Student

    📇 Harvest to Table Cards

    📇 Seed to Crop

    crayons, 16 or more

    food - can of corn

    paper, colored construction, 12"x12"

    Elmer's Glue-All

    scissors, round-end safety

    yarn

Optional

    "Picture Library: Farm Machinery" by R.J. Stephen, Franklin Watts

    "Farming" by Gail Gibbons

    "The Farm" by Stuart A. Kallen

Keywords and Pronunciation

harvesting : Gathering a crop. The farmer is harvesting the wheat.

packaging : Specially wrapping or enclosing a product. Packaging corn takes place at a factory.

processing : Preparing a crop for packaging. The workers are processing the corn.

LEARN
Activity 1. Optional: Optional Lesson Instructions *(Online)*

This lesson is OPTIONAL. It is provided for students who seek enrichment or extra practice. You may skip this lesson.

If you choose to skip this lesson, then go to the Plan or Lesson Lists page and mark this lesson "Skipped" in order to proceed to the next lesson in the course.

Activity 2. Optional: Type of Farm *(Online)*

Activity 3. Optional: Harvest to Table *(Online)*

Activity 4. Optional: Photo Book Review *(Online)*

Activity 5. Optional: Farm Machines *(Online)*

Activity 6. Optional: Life on the Farm *(Online)*

Activity 7. Optional: Visit a Farm or County Fair *(Online)*

Harvest to Table

Color and cut out the cards.

Cut

Seed to Crop Review

Cut out and place the cards in the correct order.

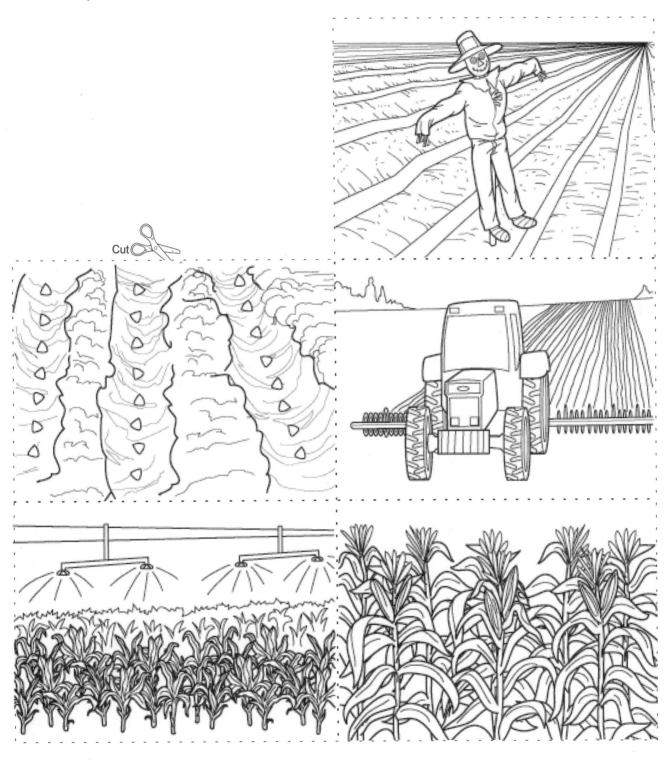

Student Guide
Lesson 1: How Things Move

Make things move with pushes and pulls. See how fast a car will move with a big push. Find out what types of objects a magnet will pick up. Use magnets to push and pull. Watch magnetism work through glass, cloth, paper, and water.

Lesson Objectives

- Describe an object's position.
- Tell how an object has moved using position words.

PREPARE

Approximate lesson time is 45 minutes.

Advance Preparation

- For this science lesson, you will need to set up an open area to resemble the setting of the story "A Day at the Petting Zoo." You may wish to do this activity outside. You will need to represent the following:

- · A fence for your student to look through

- · Two types of stuffed animals behind the fence, one for your student to pet and one for him to "feed"

- · A hat that might look like a souvenir from a petting zoo

- · Two other stuffed animals set side by side so your student can walk between them.

Materials

For the Student
  - Changing Places
  - A Day At The Petting Zoo
    household items - props for story (10)
    stuffed animals
    table
    toys - small (6)
Optional
    ball - small (6)
    cups, plastic - large (9)
    food - candy
    pencils, no. 2
    paper

Keywords and Pronunciation

motion : A change of place or position. Even though we told the dog to "stay," it made a motion toward the plate of grilled hamburgers.

position : A place or location. Because the dog kept getting closer, we changed the position of the hamburgers to the top of the refrigerator.

LEARN
Activity 1: Changing Places *(Online)*

Activity 2: Get in Position *(Online)*

Activity 3: What Moved? *(Online)*

ASSESS

Lesson Assessment: How Things Move (*Online*)

You will complete an offline assessment covering the main objectives of this lesson. Your learning coach will score this assessment.

LEARN
Activity 4: Find the Treasure *(Online)*

Name _____   Date _____

Changing Places

Circle what has moved in each picture.

Name _____   Date _____

A Day at the Petting Zoo

Read the story and act out the underlined movements of the title character. Fill in the blanks with the names of the stuffed animals you use to tell the story.

Today Jamie went to the petting zoo.

She <u>walked next</u> to an adult while looking at the animals.

She <u>looked through</u> a fence to see the _____. They made her laugh! She petted one of them with her left hand.

She got to feed a _____!
First she held out her <u>right</u> hand.
Then she <u>reached under</u> the fence.
She put her <u>right</u> hand under the _____'s chin so it could eat from her hand. It's tongue tickled her palm.

Jamie stopped at the petting zoo gift store to buy a special hat. The hat had the name of the petting zoo on the front. She <u>put the hat on top of</u> her head.

When it was time to leave, Jamie had to <u>walk between</u> the _____ and the _____. She learned that they like to follow children around petting zoos!

Lesson Assessment

How Things Move

1. Which way did the flag move, DOWN the pole or UP to the top of the pole?

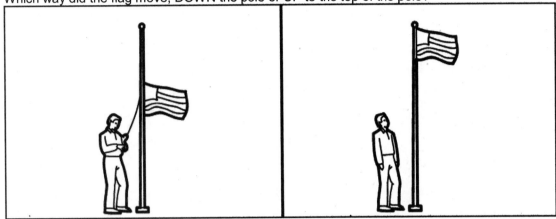

2. In which picture is the basketball OVER the net?

3. Choose the picture that shows the car to the LEFT of the house.

Student Guide
Lesson 2: Pushes and Pulls

Lesson Objectives
- Demonstrate how pushes and pulls can make things move.
- Explain that big pushes can make things go faster than small pushes.

PREPARE

Approximate lesson time is 45 minutes.

Materials
For the Student
crayons, 16 or more
pencils, no. 2
paper
tape, masking
toys - toy car
cardboard, sheets
scissors, round-end safety
string

Keywords and Pronunciation
pull : To make something move by tugging on it. The girl used the string to pull the toy train across the floor.
push : To make something move by pressing against it. Push the chair across the room.

LEARN
Activity 1: Two Ways to Move *(Online)*

Activity 2: Push and Pull Hunt *(Online)*

Activity 3: Racing Away *(Online)*

ASSESS

Lesson Assessment: Pushes and Pulls (*Online*)
You will complete an offline assessment covering the main objectives of this lesson. Your learning coach will score this assessment.

LEARN
Activity 4: Pull Toy (Online)

Lesson Assessment

Pushes and Pulls

1. Move the toy car to bring it towards you. Did you use a push or pull?

2. Gently move the toy car away from you. Did you use a push or pull?

3. How can you make the car move away from you very fast?

Student Guide
Lesson 3: A New Way to Push and Pull

Lesson Objectives

- Show that magnets attract some things made of metal.
- Recognize that magnets are strongest at the ends, at their poles.
- Demonstrate how magnets can attract and repel each other with pushes and pulls.

PREPARE

Approximate lesson time is 45 minutes.

Advance Preparation

- For this science lesson, gather the following items for your student to test with a magnet: five large paper clips or binder clips, five small paperclips, two nails, a metal spoon, a wooden or plastic spoon, a stuffed toy, a plastic toy, aluminum foil, a cloth, keys, scissors, a piece of jewelry. Select other items that your student would enjoy testing.
- Be sure you have a pair of magnets with poles identified with N and S or with a white dot. Your student will need to distinguish between the same and opposite ends of the magnets.

Materials

For the Student

    paper clips

    eraser, Pink Pearl

    foil, aluminum

    magnet, bar, pair

    nail

    pan, baking

    pencils, no. 2

    household items - cloth, jewelry, and keys

    paper clips - small and large (5)

    penny

    scissors, round-end safety

    spoon - metal & wooden or plastic (2)

    toys - plastic and stuffed

    tape, clear

    toys - cars (2)

Optional

    toys - stuffed and plastic

    dowel - wood

    magnet - ring (2)

    "First Step Science: My Magnet" by Fiona Pragoff

Keywords and Pronunciation

attract : to pull toward; magnets attract paper clips, which stick to them

magnet : An object that attracts iron or steel. If you drop a bunch of paper clips, you can use a magnet to pick them up quickly.

magnetic pole : One of two regions on a magnet, usually near the ends, where the magnet's strength is greatest. If you put a magnet into a pile of paper clips, more clips will stick around the poles than in the middle.

repel : to push away; like, or same, poles of magnets repel each other and move apart

---

LEARN
Activity 1: A New Way to Pull (Online)
Safety
Do not use magnets near a computer or other electronics such as televisions, VCRs, or radios.

Activity 2: What Sticks to Magnets? (Online)

Activity 3: Magnets Can Push, Too (Online)

Activity 4: Magnet Review (Online)

ASSESS

Lesson Assessment: A New Way to Push and Pull (Online)
You will complete an offline assessment covering the main objectives of this lesson. Your learning coach will score this assessment.

LEARN
Activity 5: Floating in Air (Online)

Activity 6: My Magnet (Online)

Lesson Assessment

A New Way to Push and Pull

1. Place a magnet next to a nail and a plastic or wooden spoon. Which one can the magnet pull?

2. Use the bar magnet to attract several paper clips. Where are the most paper clips stuck to the magnet, in the middle or at the ends?

3. Set up two bar magnets so they will pull or attract each other.

4. Set up two bar magnets so they will push or repel each other.

Student Guide
Lesson 4: Magnets Are Everywhere

Lesson Objectives

- Identify ways people use magnets.
- Explain that magnets can work through certain objects.

PREPARE

Approximate lesson time is 45 minutes.

Materials

For the Student

    pencils, no. 2

    paper

    paper clips

    jar - glass

    magnet, bar, pair

    bowl

    household items - cloth

    water

Optional

    string

    📖 Another Day at the Petting Zoo

    📖 The Petting Zoo

    books (8)

    cardboard, sheets

    scissors, round-end safety

    tape, clear

LEARN

Activity 1: How Much Do You Know About Magnets? *(Online)*

Safety

Do not use magnets near the computer and other electronics such as televisions, VCRs, or radios.

Activity 2: Magnet Hunt *(Online)*

Activity 3: Work Through It *(Online)*

Activity 4: Another Day at the Petting Zoo *(Online)*

ASSESS
Lesson Assessment: Magnets Are Everywhere (*Online*)
You will complete an offline assessment covering the main objectives of this lesson. Your learning coach will score this assessment.

LEARN
Activity 5: Magnetic Trains *(Online)*

Name _____   Date _____

Another Day at the Petting Zoo

Read this stoy aloud, giving special emphasis to the underlined portions. Pause at the end of each sentence with an underlined phrase so your child can more Jenna in the way that is described..

Today Jenna went to the petting zoo.

She <u>walked next</u> to an adult while looking at the animals.

She <u>looked through</u> a fence to see the _____. They made her laugh! She petted one of them with her left hand.

She got to feed a _____!
First she held out her <u>right</u> hand.
Then she <u>reached under</u> the fence.
She put her <u>right hand</u> under the _____'s chin so it could eat from her hand. It's tongue tickled her palm.

Jenna stopped at the petting zoo gift store to buy a special hat. The hat had the name of the petting zoo on the front. She <u>put the hat on top of</u> her head.

When it was time to leave, Jenna had to <u>walk between</u> the _____ and the _____. She learned that they like to follow children around petting zoos!

Gift Shop

exit

Welcome to the Petting Zoo

Name _____   Date _____

The Petting Zoo

Tape the picture of The Petting Zoo to a cardboard sheet. Lay the cardboard sheet on top of a pile of books high enough to move your hand around underneath. Then you are ready to work with these figures.

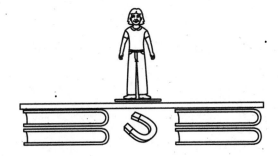

First, cut out the figure of Jenna. Tape the paper clip in the box.

Now, fold on the dotted line. repeat the procedure for Jenna's father.

Now, the figure can be moved over the board. Make certain that the magnet is just under the paper clip so that the figure can be moved by magnetism.

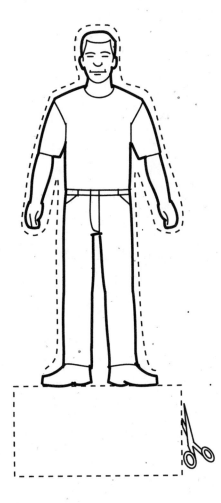

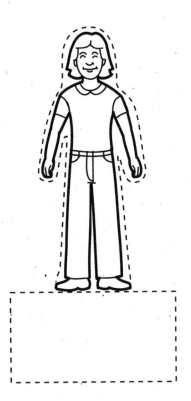

Name _____ Date _____

Lesson Assessment

Magnets Are Everywhere

1. Which does a magnet in a refrigerator door do--keep the door closed or keep the door open?

2. If you dropped a lot of sewing pins or needles on the floor, what could you use to pick them up--a magnet or a pencil?

3. Could you use a magnet to get a paper clip out of a bowl of water?

4. Could you use a magnet to make a paper clip move across paper?

Student Guide
Lesson 1: Day and Night

See just how big our closest star, the sun, really is compared to Earth. Learn about the fanciful patterns, known as constellations, formed by stars in the night sky. Create your own moonscape with sand, flour, cocoa powder, and a marble. Then meet some famous astronauts, including Neil Armstrong and Sally Ride.

Lesson Objectives

- Explain that day and night are a result of the spinning of the Earth.

PREPARE

Approximate lesson time is 45 minutes.

Advance Preparation

- Gather magazines in which your student can find pictures of daytime and nighttime activities.

Materials

For the Student

🖳 Day and Night

  1-hole punch

  crayons, 16 or more

  marker, black permanent, non-toxic

  paper, colored construction, 12"x12" - black

  plates, paper

  Elmer's Glue-All

  flashlight

  newspaper - or magazines

  paper

  scissors, round-end safety

  stapler

  tape, clear

  yarn

Optional

  clay

  globe, inflatable

  magazines

  balloon

  glitter

  stickers

LEARN
Activity 1: Day and Night *(Online)*

Activity 2: It's in the Spin *(Online)*

ASSESS
Lesson Assessment: Day and Night (*Online*)

You will complete an offline assessment covering the main objectives of this lesson. Your learning coach will score this assessment.

LEARN
Activity 3. Optional: View from the Sun *(Online)*

Name   Date

Day and Night

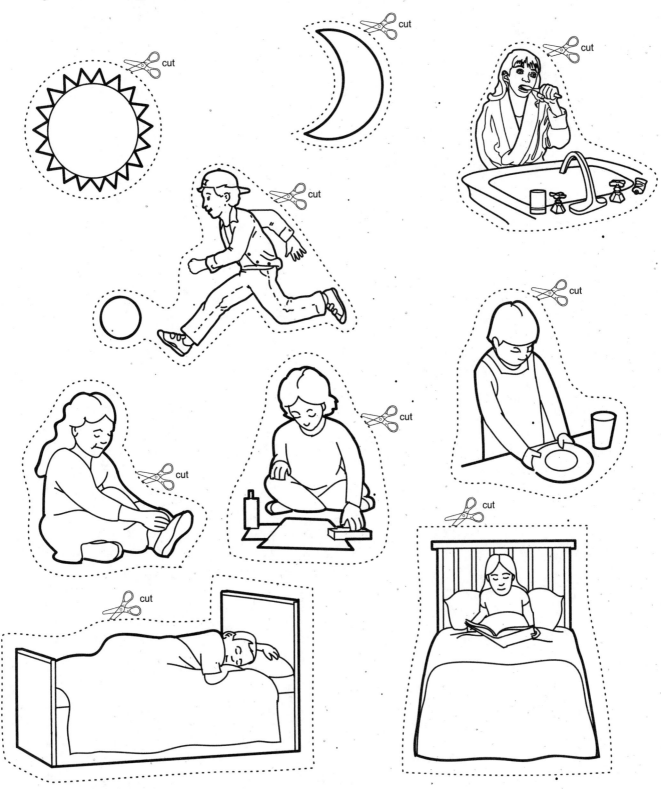

Lesson Assessment

Day and Night

1. What causes the sky to get dark at night--the Earth spinning or someone covering the Earth with a blanket?

2. Point to the letter that shows the nighttime side of the Earth.

Student Guide
Lesson 2: The Closest Star

Lesson Objectives

- Recognize that stars are very far away.
- Compare the size of the sun to the size of the Earth.
- State that the sun is a star.

PREPARE

Approximate lesson time is 45 minutes.

Advance Preparation

- For this science lesson, cut a piece of yarn about 25 feet long. When you connect the ends of the yarn to make a circle, the circle's diameter should measure about 8 feet.

Materials

For the Student

meter stick, 100 cm

scissors, round-end safety

toys - marble (2cm in diameter), toy car

yarn - 25 ft

Optional

1-hole punch

paper, colored construction, 12"x12" - red, yellow, orange, white

pencils, no. 2

index cards, 4" x 6"

markers, colored, 8 or more

newspaper - or magazines

stapler

tape, clear

yarn

toys - marbles, 2 cm in diameter (10)

LEARN
Activity 1: Looking Up (Online)

Activity 2: The Sun Is a Star *(Online)*

Activity 3. Optional: Here Comes the Sun *(Online)*

ASSESS

Lesson Assessment: The Closest Star *(Online)*

You will complete an offline assessment covering the main objectives of this lesson. Your learning coach will score this assessment.

LEARN

Activity 4. Optional: How Many Earths? *(Online)*

Activity 5. Optional: A Star up Close *(Online)*

Lesson Assessment

The Closest Star

1. Which is bigger--the Earth or the sun?

2. Which is a star--the Earth or the sun?

3. Are the stars you see at night close to Earth or far away from Earth?

4. What is the closest star to Earth--the sun or the moon?

Student Guide
Lesson 3: Star Patterns

Lesson Objectives

- Recognize that groups of stars form shapes in the sky called constellations.
- Identify the Big Dipper and Little Dipper constellations.

PREPARE

Approximate lesson time is 45 minutes.

Advance Preparation

- Before this science lesson, remove both ends of an empty coffee can, making sure you leave no sharp edges. Line the inside of the can with black paper.

- Have your student look at the night sky. You can see more details when you are away from streetlights, floodlights, or other city lights.

- Direct your student to look for the following:

- · Bright stars and not-so-bright stars

- · Groups of stars

- · Stars that you could play "connect the dots" with to make a shape or design

- Tell your student that you will not see stars move in the night sky. If you see streaks of light or moving lights, they may be airplanes or meteors. Reinforce the idea that stars are much too far away to touch or visit.

Materials

For the Student

"The Big Dipper" by Franklyn Branley (ISBN 0-06-445100-3)

cooking equipment - soup ladle

Optional

ball - large and small (2)

cardboard, sheets

food - black pepper

nail

pencils, no. 2

can, tin - coffee, bottom removed

flashlight

tape, clear

paper, colored construction, 12"x12" - black

chalk - white

Elmer's Glue-All

glitter

household items - toothpaste

newspaper - or magazines

Keywords and Pronunciation

constellation : a group of stars that form a shape in the sky; the stars in the constellation The Big Dipper take the shape of a water dipper with a handle and bowl

---

LEARN

Activity 1: Shapes in the Sky *(Online)*

Activity 2: The Big Dipper *(Online)*

Activity 3: Make a Constellation *(Online)*

Safety

Do not let your student punch the holes in the cardboard with the nail.

Activity 4. Optional: Find the Big Dipper *(Online)*

ASSESS

Lesson Assessment: Star Patterns (*Online*)

You will complete an offline assessment covering the main objectives of this lesson. Your learning coach will score this assessment.

LEARN

Activity 5. Optional: Constellations *(Online)*

Activity 6. Optional: Night Observations *(Online)*

Lesson Assessment

Star Patterns

1. **Turn to page 30 in *The Big Dipper*. Read the following to your student:**
   Point to the Big Dipper and the Little Dipper in the picture.

2. What is a constellation--a group of moons or a group of stars?

3. Do some people think that groups of stars look like animals and other shapes?

Student Guide
Lesson 4: Biography: Neil Armstrong

Lesson Objectives
- Identify Neil Armstrong as the first person to walk on the moon.
- Name some items that the astronauts brought back from the first trip to the moon.

PREPARE

Approximate lesson time is 45 minutes.

Materials
For the Student
>
> crayons, 16 or more
>
> pencils, no. 2
>
> markers, colored, 8 or more
>
> paper
>
> scissors, round-end safety

Optional
>
> index cards, 4" x 6"
>
> paper, drawing, 12" x 18"

Keywords and Pronunciation
astronaut : A person who travels in space. Astronaut Neil Armstrong flew to the moon.

observe : To look carefully at something. The girl observed the moon through her telescope.

LEARN
Activity 1: Up and Away *(Online)*

Activity 2: Neil Armstrong *(Online)*

Activity 3: Postcard from the Moon *(Online)*

ASSESS

Lesson Assessment: Biography: Neil Armstrong (*Online*)
You will complete an offline assessment covering the main objectives of this lesson. Your learning coach will score this assessment.

LEARN

Activity 4. Optional: National Air and Space Museum *(Online)*

Activity 5. Optional: Earth from the Moon *(Online)*

Lesson Assessment

Biography: Neil Armstrong

1. Who was the first man to walk on the moon--Neil Armstrong or Edwin Aldrin?

2. What did Neil Armstrong bring back from the moon to study?

Student Guide
Lesson 5: On the Surface of the Moon

Lesson Objectives

- Describe the surface of the moon as dusty, rocky, and covered with craters.
- Explain why people cannot live on the moon.

PREPARE

Approximate lesson time is 45 minutes.

Advance Preparation

- Find an area in which you do not mind making a mess. Spread newspaper on a flat surface in that area.

Materials

For the Student

    food - cocoa powder and flour

    pan, baking

    sand

    newspaper - or magazines

    tape, masking

    toys - marble

Optional

    "What the Moon is Like" by Franklyn M.Branley

    binoculars

Keywords and Pronunciation

crater : A hole or pit in the ground. Rocks from space hit the moon's surface, leaving many deep craters.

LEARN
Activity 1: How We Observe the Moon *(Online)*

Activity 2: A Splash of Rock *(Online)*

ASSESS

Lesson Assessment: On the Surface of the Moon (*Online*)

You will complete an offline assessment covering the main objectives of this lesson. Your learning coach will score this assessment.

Lesson Assessment

On the Surface of the Moon

1. Which is a picture of the moon?

2. Point to a crater in the picture.

3. Point to the rocks in the picture.

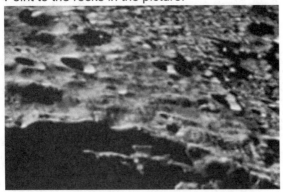

4. Why can't people live on the moon?

Student Guide
Lesson 6: Biography: Sally Ride

Lesson Objectives

- Compare life on Earth to how astronauts must live while traveling in space.
- Identify Sally Ride as the first American woman to fly into space.

PREPARE

Approximate lesson time is 45 minutes.

Materials

For the Student

plastic sandwich bags, zipper-closed

household items - large plastic container

paper - scraps and crumpled

Optional

drink mix, powdered - milk or juice

tray, Styrofoam, clean

fruits - dried

string

envelope

pencils, no. 2

stamps

markers, colored, 8 or more

paper

Keywords and Pronunciation

space shuttle : A spacecraft on which astronauts can live for months and return to Earth. The first space shuttle, *Columbia,* blasted off and returned to Earth in 1981.

LEARN
Activity 1: Space Is a Busy Place *(Online)*

Activity 2: Sally Ride *(Online)*

Activity 3: Life in Space *(Online)*
Safety
This activity involves working with food. Before beginning, check with your doctor, if necessary, to assess whether your student will have any allergic reaction to this food.

Activity 4. Optional: Remember Sally Ride *(Online)*

ASSESS
Lesson Assessment: Biography: Sally Ride (*Online*)
You will complete an offline assessment covering the main objectives of this lesson. Your learning coach will score this assessment.

LEARN
Activity 5. Optional: Write to Sally Ride *(Online)*

Activity 6. Optional: The Space Shuttle *(Online)*

Lesson Assessment

Biography: Sally Ride

1. This is a picture of the first American woman to fly into space. What is her name?

2. What do astronauts do with handles and straps in the space shuttle--use them to move or hang clothes on them?

3. Do you need handles and straps to keep you from floating around on Earth?

4. Name one way that a day in your life on Earth is different from an astronaut's day in space.

Answer Keys

Lesson Assessment Answer Key

What About Weather?

Part 1

Answers:

Review your student's answers to the *My Weather Chart* activity and enter the number of points earned based on the following criteria:

Did your student observe and record weather conditions correctly on his My Weather Chart?	10 points
Did your student use the correct symbols to record weather conditions on his My Weather Chart?	10 points
Total:	

Part 2

Answers:

1. Answers may vary but could include sunny, cloudy, hot, cold, rainy, snowy, or windy.

2. Accept any reasonable answer.

3. the picture of the boy in the swimsuit

4. Answers will vary but could include a coat, mittens, hat, boots, sweaters, etc.

Lesson Assessment Answer Key

The Sun's Up

Answers:

1. warm

2. It would dry.

3. into the air

4. Answers will vary.

Lesson Assessment Answer Key

As the Wind Blows

Answers:

1. Wind or moving air would cause the objects to move.

2. wind

3. The objects will be moving or blowing away.

4. Your student should draw a windsock with streamers still and a windsock showing the streamers to be moving as if by a breeze.

Lesson Assessment Answer Key

Watching the Clouds Go By

Answers:

1. Clouds are made of water.

2. The wind makes clouds move.

3. no

4. the picture on the left

Lesson Assessment Answer Key

Raindrops and Rainbows

Answers:

1. rain

2. a rainbow

3. Answers may vary but can include red, orange, yellow, green, blue, indigo, and violet.

Lesson Assessment Answer Key

Weather Watch

Answers:

1. a tornado

2. rain

3. rain

4. B.

Lesson Assessment Answer Key

Falling for Fall

Answers:

1. B.

2. cooler

3. gather, store, or hide nuts

Lesson Assessment Answer Key

Winter Wonderland

Answers:

1. winter

2. B.

3. snow

Lesson Assessment Answer Key

Animals in Winter

Answers:

1. sleeping all winter long

2. grass

3. digging under the snow for bits of grass and plants to eat

4. migrating

5. bird, butterfly

Lesson Assessment Answer Key

Spring Has Sprung

Answers:

1. warmer

2. Answers may vary but could include: the weather becomes warmer and wetter, and the days become longer. These changes help flowers grow.

3. B.

4. Answers will vary, but might include: build a nest, get ready for their babies, migrate, or wake from hibernation.

Lesson Assessment Answer Key

Summer Sun

Answers:

1. B.

2. swim in a pool

3. summer

4. fall

5. yes

Lesson Assessment Answer Key

The Shape of the Earth

Answers:

1. Earth

2. sphere or round

3. During the lesson, your student should have been able to locate the North Pole, South Pole and equator on a globe.

Lesson Assessment Answer Key

The Earth's Surface

Answers:

1. land and water

2. more water

3. oceans

4. continents

Lesson Assessment Answer Key

Land Shapes

Answers:

1. a hill

2. a valley

3. an island

Lesson Assessment Answer Key

Bodies of Water

Answers:

1. a river

2. a lake

3. an ocean

Lesson Assessment Answer Key

Rocks and Soil

Answers:

1. rocks and soil

2. yes

3. yes

4. During the lesson, your student should have been able to sort the gathered rocks into two groups: large and small. Your student should also have been able to sort the rocks into two groups of rough and smooth.

Name _____   Date _____

Lesson Assessment Answer Key

The Earth Gives Us So Much

Answers:

1. Answers will vary but may include pencils, paper, furniture, or boxes.

2. Answers will vary but may include swimming, boating, fishing, snorkeling, or surfing.

3. Wooden items around the home may include furniture, picture frames, cabinets, toys, wooden spoons, ladders, pianos, pencils, and paper supplies, including books and newspapers.

4. Your student should have been able to identify several of the ways water is used around the home. Also discuss some ways we use water that may be harder to identify. Plants such as vegetables need water to grow, for example, and we eat vegetables. So we also use the water found in some plants.

Lesson Assessment Answer Key

Why Should We Conserve?

Answers:

1.

2.

3. Accept any reasonable answer including: turn off the water while brushing your teeth and keep the faucet turned off so it doesn't drip.

4. Accept any reasonable answer including: turn off lights or other electrical items when they are not in use and or think about what is wanted before opening the refrigerator.

Lesson Assessment Answer Key

Is There a Solution to Pollution?

Answers:

1. illustration 1

2. illustration 3

3. Accept any reasonable answer, such as picking up trash, making sure trash gets thrown away.

Lesson Assessment Answer Key

Reduce, Reuse, Recycle

Answers:

1. Answers will vary but may include recycling, using items more than once, or choosing objects that can be used many times rather than once and then discarded

Lesson Assessment Answer Key

Biography: Rachel Carson

Answers:

1. nature

2. Items that might be used for the drawings or rubbings include leaves, twigs and weeds.

Lesson Assessment Answer Key

How Things Move

Answers:

1. up to the top

2.

3.

Lesson Assessment Answer Key

Pushes and Pulls

Answers:

1. pull

2. push

3. with a hard push

Lesson Assessment Answer Key

A New Way to Push and Pull

Answers:

1. the nail

2. the ends

3. Opposite poles should be facing each other.

4. Like poles should be facing each other.

Lesson Assessment Answer Key

Magnets Are Everywhere

Answers:

1. It keeps the door closed.

2. a magnet

3. yes

4. yes

Lesson Assessment Answer Key

Day and Night

Answers:

1. the Earth spinning

2. A

Lesson Assessment Answer Key

The Closest Star

Answers:

1. the sun

2. the sun

3. far away

4. the sun

Lesson Assessment Answer Key

Star Patterns

Answers:

1. Your student should be able to identify pictures of the Big Dipper and Little Dipper on the page.

2. a group of stars

3. yes

Lesson Assessment Answer Key

Biography: Neil Armstrong

Answers:

1. Neil Armstrong

2. moon rocks and soil

Lesson Assessment Answer Key

On the Surface of the Moon

Answers:

1.

2. A crater is a large pit in the moon's surface.

3. Rocks are the large, broken up pieces on the moon.

4. Answers may vary but should include one of the following: no air, no water, no food, overly hot temperatures, or overly cold temperatures.

Lesson Assessment Answer Key

Biography: Sally Ride

Answers:

1. Sally Ride

2. use them to move

3. no

4. Answers may vary but could include these: difference in dealing with gravity, throwing trash away, going to the bathroom, trying to walk, etc.